PENTAMENTALY

A-BINGO

Noetic Notion… nourishment necessary now!

(APHAERESIS)

ALLITERATION

AuthorHouse™
1663 Liberty Drive
Bloomington, IN 47403
www.authorhouse.com
Phone: 833-262-8899

Because of the dynamic nature of the Internet, any web addresses or links contained in this book may have changed
since publication and may no longer be valid. The views expressed in this work are solely those of the author and do not
necessarily reflect the views of the publisher, and the publisher hereby disclaims any responsibility for them.

This book is printed on acid-free paper.

ISBN: 978-1-4634-0473-4 (sc)
ISBN: 978-1-4969-1875-8 (e)

Print information available on the last page.

Published by AuthorHouse 08/01/2022

authorHOUSE®

HEADING

PENTAMENTALY A-BINGO- www.AuthorHouse.com- (HEADING)-Which way will "WORDS" work for us? A book of alliteration can help people see new "WORDS" that is beneficial to intellectual thought. In the initial learning process people might have trouble understanding "WORDS" that aren't well known! I hope that one can soon learn some "WORDS" needed to provide an abundant expansion of knowledge essential to enjoying a prosperous life. All facets of living include some knowledge of understanding. Have fun reading these "WORDS"of alliteration too initiate one's enhanced educational quest.

Here are some definitions of this wondrous word, "pentament" that's helped me repose to compose, NOETIC NOTION. Without the pentament this book would have been just another worthless wordy book. With the use of the pentament the syntactical connection of words is neatly found. Why learn the definition of one word, when people can orderly learn five at once? This direct approach to reading words should help increase the intelligence of anyone wanting to learn! To conjoin the morpheme "penta" with the morpheme "ment" was a radical logical calculated connection creating convenient crystallization (C). The government has a pentagon to protect America. Now Americans can perceive paradigm pentament projected perfections (P). The book can easily enrich ethical expansion economically (E). The alliterative writings are a proper source of word connection to increase the vocabulary of anyone that wants to learn. An alphabetical connection of words will save fumbling through all the pages of the dictionary! The innovative inception of some revolutionary comforts of life was invented by lazy people. If everyone was energetic there won't be any new comforts of life. Here are some different direct dogmatic defending definitions (D-pentament) of the pentament. The character of this word can help fight off an ignorance of anyone to build classic charisma.

- Pentament- Primordial prose that includes the original concept conclusive concentrated consecutive conjunction of five words alphabetically aphaeresis, alliteration void repetition.

- Pentament- The resulting artifact product of a literal alliteration process of five consecutive words starting with the same letter teaching an origin of historical linguistics.

- Pentament- The act, fact, practical artful process of five consecutive alliterative words causing historical linguistics, Vernacular English.

- Pentament- Teaching an idiomatically syntactical alliteration connection of five different words that start with the same letter to institute historical linguistics.

- Pentament- A alphabetical alliteration of five consecutive words teaching historical linguistics to instill instrumental intuitive intellect into one that wants to know.

Thanks to us, we have this Symposium. With encouraging endorsements this book could help to educate an ignorant America. My tenor on this earth is almost through the rest of the book of alliteration is up to those who want to live in a society of humane intellectual equality. The poor indigenous of America are at an acute (A-pentament) disadvantage learning, they can't afford books. Maybe this book can be an affordable foundation of proper education? Teach words that have to be taught, why live one's life in naught? Help make one's life be what it can be, by being at least as intelligent as me! First I need to tell these three things that (T) are true, I don't spell well, can't write right, know no English. These are three negative things that I overcome to write this book. Now I encourage one to be what one can be even if one doesn't learn it all from me. Trying to be wise, using good judgment, with great love and respect from my wit, please learn it. In other words, SAGE REVERENCE WISEGUY JACK. The introductions of the "pentament" are now through let's get to it reading a knowledgeable book that jogs one's mind too wit.

INTRODUCTION TO-NOETIC NOTION…NOURISHMENT NECESSARY NOW

There are six reasons why this book was composed. Everyone has a reason to exist with this book mine. My three (wacky ways with writing will) be mentioned first. To correlate credible balance three positive postulations will be written to corroborate composition of the book. Later a synthesis of alliteration like (W) above is simply shown.

(1) don't spell well (2) can't write right (3) know no English (4) knowledgeable of the definitions of most 8th grade words (5) know all mathematical calculations (6) The explicit intelligible academic exposition of words will be initiated with an opinion of interjections to construct a form of historical linguistics alliteration to ordain all literate.

With the use of "WORDS" in logical order this book will grasp a stabilized language equal to historical linguistics, Vernacular English. The British English that is in most books nowadays is repetition with an abundance of the iteration of the same idea in different "WORDS" which is confusing to the average student that is reluctant to learn. Education can teach something that jogs an atrophied mind into existence sometime? What "WORDS" do children learn during school nowadays, ah not (about any at all ay)?

Using a direct approach to the indoctrination of new "WORDS" the poor children of America will be more susceptible to learn. I reckon that kids see "WORDS" to know them. The epoch "WORDS" learned is of their own reckoning! Everyone in the universe is a universe of their own. We constitute a human quintessential essence relevance of this universe. Let's teach universal Vernacular English instead of repetitious British English. Vernacular "WORDS" from mother's tongue is what's written. Transferring of this initial vocabulary is a foundation of primordial education. Having the vocabulary of one improves a vocabulary of none. Learn "WORDS" to incite all crucial nutritious learning!

This doctrine of alliteration will entice the learning of new "WORDS" which is essential to the humanities of futuristic education. Them "WORDS" should be shown to them to be known by them! This was written in poor British English to show that the recurrence of (them) is repetitious which is to be avoided in, NOETIC NOTION… NOURISHMENT NECESSARY NOW! To insert all "WORDS" that start with the letters A,B,I,N,G,O into this forty page book the "pentament" a new formed coined word was invented that will constitute clear continuous constructive concentration (C-pentament). Being the old vain man that I am this vital divergent dogmatic dialectical decorum display (D-pentament) can transfer inspired indigenous ingenuous intellectual inflectional (I-pentament) accidence into one that reads this adept instruction. Will "WORDS" work?

Children can learn new "WORDS" to foster development of their educational lives. British English is faulted prolix with excessive ambiguity that teaches children the infected intelligence of abundant repetitions. Children should be taught new exciting "WORDS" to keep them interested in education. The acronym of "FANBOYS", are the seven coordinating conjunctions that will be limited. The conjunctions, For, And, Nor, But, Or, Yet, So. These conjunctions slow down one's line of thought. A perfect thought can assume this jot! With the learning of new "WORDS" education will be a fun filled vacation instead of vocation. Humanities have to be taught to all that enter 8th grade! This propositional legacy should be firmly upheld? To not teach children humanities is to not teach children anything at all. Epochal historical linguistics assistance will help America to be number one. Please look at the dictionary with wit which tells which witch is which.

INTRODUCTION TO- NOETIC NOTION... NOURISHMENT NECESSARY NOW

Five acronyms will be used in this introduction to help explain the contents of the book

1. (CAST)-concise, abridged, synopsis, tersely=make a short story of language

2. (Spa)-Socrates, Plato, Aristotle=470 B.C.-2009 A.D. my vernacular language

3. (Wafer)-Water, air, fire, earth, rudiments=ultimate adhesive essence of life

4. (See)-substance, elements, essence=the composition of all matter in the universe

5. (FANBOYS)-For, And, Nor, But, Or, Yet, So=these are intellectual infections that aren't used in this introduction. FANBOYS are a weak link of my intelligence

These next two groups of sentences about the book are similar, said in different words.

(1) Noetic Notion will form a (Cast) to the relaxed educated (Spa) of a (Wafer) of knowledge to (See) if literature could teach new esoteric words without the use of excessive (FANBOYS). Noetic Notions alliteration of esoteric words should help make all literate? This is why I construe teaching vernacular.

(2) Noetic Notion endeavors understanding of dialectical exclamations to form a historical linguistics sharp synopsis syntax synthesis subsequently (S-pentament) involves inserting indigenous indoctrination instilling (I-pentament) opinions that will help develop inflectional accidence. Noetic Notions alliteration of esoteric words should help make all literate? This is why I construe teaching vernacular.

It would be wonderful if children could relax to learn, maybe write new found words to improve inert incomplete intelligence. The rendering of new words helps the unavoidable communications with others in this congested world.

Humanities should be taught in Liberal Arts classes during the 8th grade. The vocation education is an infection of education that has to be eradicated. To teach children humanities should be the foundational roots of all education. The lack of learning is due to limited liberal literal lectures leaving (L-pentament) youngsters afraid of a proper education. America has to make education more fun to increase the basic intellect of everyone. Give kid's something they want to read that motivates provident accidence to increase their vocabulary. It would be better to have sense rather than cents. If a person has sense they will eventually receive more cents. Remember the old adage. Feed a person a fish to keep them alive one day. Teach a person how to fish to keep them fishing their lives away every day!

All words in Noetic Notion came from an 8th grade dictionary. I claim that I'm as intelligent as most 8th graders. If 8th graders were as intelligent as I am they could excel in future adult life. This book is a genuine quality attempt to initiate something intelligent to interfere with the ignorance of this under educated United States of America. The only degree that I am graced with is one of intelligence!

Noetic Notion is a nostrum transferable knowledge from me to anyone wanting to combat unwanted indecent idiotic institutionalized illogical ignorance (I-pentament). Noetic Notion is a pivotal interjectional biographical history of human interactions with American government. This book is a collection of some interesting exclamations of events which occurred during my 62years of life. In other words which are true, this is my life to you, Sage Reverence Wiseguy Jack.

NOETIC NOTION is sub-titled PENTAMENTALY A-BINGO, which is the mode that these letters, A, B, I, N, G, O, are wrote in. The arrangement of these six short stories should show (S-pentament) a comprehensive model of the composition of future books of alliteration. If one were to rewrite these stories in British English instead of Vernacular English, it would take 105,000 words instead of 21,000. The initial intelligence to read what was written will waken whimsical (W) notions toward reading that always have been obscure. The locution of this wording wakes up parts of the brain to perceive word functions. Poor kid's that want to be rappers should really be enthused with this particular type of reference. There is hope that these writings will inspire one to learn new words. The intellect to read this new book is similar to other books. After one is exposed to this book's type of writing one won't be afraid of words, one will become aware words are grains of the cereal of life, grams of knowledge. Sudden enlightenment that I knew the definitions of almost all 8th grade words is why there is a book! I went to college to be an electrician; I know math, algebra, geometry, trigonometry, calculus, why intuitive word knowledge? Words are rudimentary elements of knowledge that were accidentally instilled into me. These words are the vernacular language learned from my indigent parents to share with all. The substance of words emerged as an acknowledging authorship authorizing action (A) to initiate reforming reclusive education. Language can enable effective eternal epic enforcement empowering equal efficient eminent eloquent education (E). I urge one to have fun, learn to read, read to learn. Yearn to learn! Before I finish this long distance run of life, I want to share the knowledge of words with whoever wants wit (W) to share it. Here are excerpts from the book one is bad grammar, that's me.

(A) Pg5-By setting goals for adult life when in high school adolescents can accent the absorption of great knowledge about jobs; actually amplify assurance averting aimless accomplishments. Pg11-The antecedent antics affecting the articles of discouraging most major discrimination were patriotic harmony atop altruistically axiomatic anomaly avalanche. "I have a dream we shall over-come", what the honorable.

(B) Pg15- Most zoo daze develops the betterment of the whole beautiful blooming bothersome bouncing bunch. Pg16-It was hard to breathe: I was turning blue in fear from the barrage of the biased brunt brash bigot brutality this bowlegged backwoodsman looking bumpkin of a guy was besieging upon us!

(I) Pg20-Inclusive identifying informality indicates terrorist main intentions are to indiscriminately infiltrate isolated inhabitants innocence with incapacitated ill-bred infractions of totally inharmonious violence! Pg21- Who might this mighty invulnerable illumining intimidating infiltrating interracial omnipresent interposed executioner be, as the world turns? IS ARE wrong?

(N) = (IMPROPER GRAMMAR) Pg23- Being a kind narrator are the words still navigable or should I nervously neglect being a caring, sharing neighbor and negotiate newly noble nonsensical notation? Pg26- This is why I say in a nutshell, Noetic Notion ... nourishment necessary now!

(G) Pg30- Felling gritty I could have become a gambling gamester and galloped into the ghetto to greet a gangster and gained a grandly deal from the grumpiest greediest guiltiest goriest gunman? Pg30- While in this potent geology greenery field one could look up to see the pretty birds, robins, eagles, doves, grosbeaks, grouse, gull and of course guinea fowl, grebe, gander, geese, gobblers, and the little gosling that run through the field.

PREFACE

What is that one might say, Noetic-relating to the mind-Notion-a mental idea, opinion, to inform? Aphaeresis-thee taking of a letter or syllable from the beginning of a word.

Noetic Notion . . . . . nourishment necessary now just gracefully accidentally, eclectically making an abridgment of the dictionary!! Intelligently want to inform readers that that are not the word or words that I will use. My proposition is to write this treatise "pentamentaly". In a "pentament", each letter of the alphabet is used to form a "pentament" The lucid definition is-PENTAMENT—primordial prose that includes the original concept conclusive concentrated consecutive conjunction of five words alphabetically aphaeresis, alliteration void repetition. Arduously prescribe never to use a pentament word twice within its aphaeresis pentamentaly short story. Being human there could be a peccadillo? I'll encourage anyone to take a few hours to find where I've made a mistake by using my pentamental words twice within its nominated literary pentament! It is time to read the words to consume the dictionary one letter at a time! This book will induce sage neologism! To learn new words helps daily stirring communication with others!

To make this treatise concise and precise, JKQUVWXYZ are considerably smaller in summary so they will be grouped together to form one pentament. These letters combined have the equivalent amount of words as each of the other individual letters of the alphabet, look at your dictionary. Eighteen pentamentaly assorted short stories with strict alphabetic pentament consideration. It'll probably take me to long to complete the C-pentament and S-pentaments. Being 60yrs old there won't be enough time to consume all the words that start with these two letters? Those words are 20% of the words in the dictionary, only time will tell if I make it!

This book will be written in three volumes with six chapters each. This first volume is sub-titled A-BINGO a pedagogy to my gal "Sal" and Susan my sister's or anyone that reads it? Sally somehow gets lucky at bingo and hits for $2000 or more at least twice a year! These are the first six letters that have been used up to introduce new words to inspire the use of the dictionary! Maybe with a little luck like Sally has it might be A-BINGO? My little sister Sue has cancer and is trying to recover with anything but money, she needs an idea for survival? With any luck in our lives the next two volumes will be produced at a later time? All pentament words will be highlighted in different colors or illustrated italicizes to further enhance this primordial prose.

Please enjoy this pentamentaly distinctive discernible dictionary dialectical disquisition. That that is my first (d-pentament) is an ingenious inspirational imbue interpretive introduction. Having now introduced everyone to a (I-pentament), each pentamental story will regard just the words that start with that specific letter. That that cannot be put under the (T-pentament) "that" can only be done once! Coincidently that that can be put within any other pentamental story infinitely! The stories are just MULES that carry the words that must be seen!

The aphaeresis of all words will conspicuously hold the didactics together. The dictionary will outlive everyone. Please excuse the introduction to Noetic Notion, it was written by a "Rocket Scientist", me. I'm very sorry it might be hard to understand, it all makes sense to me. Enjoy this book that shows some people new words to incite neologism. There that explains it all! If the rest of the book is ok, maybe one could write a few mules for a pentament of any choice. Learning new innovative words by accident should increase one's enthusiasm for reading! Please have fun learning the dictionary pentamentaly. Being lost for words, may I wish everyone good luck in reading these words that one should know? Yours truly, sage reverence, JACK

INTRODUCTION

Since I am an urchin Pentamentologist without tutelage, will voluntarily systematically tentatively temporize linguistic prolix proficiently. Foist extemporaneous philologically phrase uniformly explicitly extracting universal verbosity. Reduce verbiages constituencies epitomize literature logically. Instill inflection intuitively reduces abundance of archaic essential repetitious verbatim. Obviate pleonasm organically through extreme inspired dialectics.

Pentamentaly primordial prose reforms original intelligent interpretation to contract perspicuous elimination. Predispose ancient prosaic composition uniformly. Disavow essential essay revolutionize fortuitous original primordial creative summary. Impose discreet compacted inspirational implicitly affirmative intentionally aggressive irrevocable quest. Institute systematic synopsis prose alliteration indoctrination educes dictionary quantification to make all literate.

Who would have thought that that would be the word or words of thought through which I fashion this exposition? Noetic Notion will encourage providentially prepossessing elicit fabulous fanciful inscrutable circumvention dictionary diction. Noetic Notion will be a sensible interesting refined concept conclusive concentrated consecutive conjunction compendium composition. This is a (C-pentament). The dictionary irresistibly wrote in a positively polite predominately pentament prose. This is a (P-pentament). To try taking the total (T-pentament) dictionary into a simple short story satisfactory sufficient (S-pentament) to increase one's knowledge of words? This story was written to enhance the average 13yrs old kid's vocabulary!

Consequentially imperative categorical elimination of elementary eclectic subjective particles is Noetic Notion! Antecedent predetermines righteous scholastic edification. Render graciously condensed didactical pertinacious phrase. Articulate excerpt exposes habitually familiarized insignificant redundancies! Inculcation of words equitably creates distinctive organized coherent neologism. Words are for communication with the people of this world!

Please enjoy this superannuated . . . . DICTIONARY DICTION . . . .

To try to dine is fine as long as you have just a little wine? Try a pentament after dinner? I hope these short stories contract common codification clearly capable (C-pentament) to raise the essence of reading to enlighten all? Let the fruition of the pentament began—S and J a couple distinguished members of a bar. My nieces and nephews are my number one intellectual inspiration to write this book. They all told me to "dumb it down" so that they could understand?

I dedicate this book to the concentrated philosophies of the plentiful philosophers that I have read! Past "GREAT MEN and WOMEN" that it would be wonderful to emulate that I extol with my heart, soul and very fertile mind that they have nourished with dignity and pride and great wisdom! My personal list of knowledge in no particular order—Thomas Hobbs, Plato, Aristotle Confucius, Spinoza, Locke, Descartes, Hume, Socrates, Rousseau, Kant and Berkeley, Luxemburg, Goldman to name a few. Mr. Jerome Frank-Fate and Freedom (1945), a great book.

Mr. Jerome Frank was the main philosopher that got me going on this idea to write a book. If I had half his humanitarian history my book would be to incredible for any human to read or understand! He was the most admirable man that I've ever read. His books were written with well-grounded wisdom that I'll never forget. Each page had at least one word that I couldn't understand teaching ideal neologism! His works will be held in great reverence by me forever!

(PENTAMENTS)

"Mules"

Mules	Title	Theme
1—A-PENTAMENT—Educational Encouragements		Equal Rights
2—B-PENTAMENT—Zoo Daze		Fun Family Plan
3—I-PENTAMENT—World Peace		Worldly Terrorism
4—N-PENTAMENT—Those Words		To Know Words
5—G-PENTAMENT—Childs Courtesy		Manly Manners
6—O-PENTAMENT—B.P. and Me		The Oil Spill

PRELUDE:

These pentaments are chapters to a normal reader when one reads a normal writer. I never once said that I'm normal, that would be to informal. The mules (STORIES) that have been written should carry the words to increase some people's knowledge of words? If there might be an intelligent person that should disagree with me, please tell me how dumb I am in words I can understand? Understanding is 100% of our daily battle for survival! If one is a genius to know all these words just keep it to oneself to let us that are ignorant stay as such? It would be wonderful if one could teach an old man like me something that I don't know! If one can't understand, how will one know if they are right or wrong? To understand is to know. To know is to understand.

To avoid knowledge is to avoid a proper confined, defined, refined way of life! I can't understand the basic knowledge of children nowadays which is beyond reasoning? If I was as intelligent as the average graduating school kid of today when I graduated in 1968, I would have died by now! They are all shoved through school with a swiftness that superman would be proud of! I'm the inborn uncle of honor roll nieces and nephews that aren't quite up to par with me, yet I was only 2.65GPA when I left high school. Of course going to college for awhile (10yrs) might have helped to accumulate some understanding of words

or knowledge? Understanding knows!

Don't let the actions of life pass living without a touch of class. Not to be crude or rude, get one's life in gear to make a direct attempt to acquire something intelligent to be a star on the stage of one's own life. This is almost my last act, the final stage or actions of kindness to help in any way to make Americans at least half as dumb as the Japanese or the Chinese that have finally taken over our American economy!

Why hold back one's mind to become an inept inane infirm incapacitated improvising idiot? Why bow down to every country of the world with our stupid acts? People once were proud Americans! What's up, get on stage, make one's LIFE ACT quite noticeable to one that doesn't know. Help America be # one on stage, whipping the mules @ U!

(A-Pentament)

Educational Encouragements

High school education is advantageous nowadays to account for acquiring sufficient income to ascend toward supporting life's finer aspirations. High school dropouts have less ability finding work that administers enough pay toward accumulation the luxuries of life. The high school diploma or GED is the accelerator toward receiving the acquisition of decent jobs throughout this present day vast economical world. The automotive industry was thriving when I was 18 yrs old, everyone could hire in the shop with decent pay. Nowadays automation has taken control with machines actuating 80% of the automatic work. The main allotment of factory work is aimed for the acquirement to activating the amplified advances by the skilled trade's workers.

I spent 37 yrs, on skilled trades, doing electrical maintenance work for Buick Motor Division. General Motors paid for my 10yrs of college, 4yrs of my education was acquainted to studies of my apprenticeship. I received a decent wage when working, now I'm retired drawing my pension. After years of accomplished negotiations the union has supplied me with accessory retirement benefits also! The approach applying for factory work is to be industrious apprentices within the trades for the applicant's adequacy acceptance. I had 1.6 GPA when hired @ GM!

To avoid anticipating actual factory work, let education achievement guarantee that the appropriate job desired will be yours to appreciate. Factory work is the only job affluence that I had the acquaintance with. I must admit there could be better jobs. Being educated by the college or academy is the auspicious way toward adopting admittance for admired job approval. By setting goals for adult life when in high school adolescents can accent the absorption of great knowledge about jobs, actually amplify assurance averting aimless accomplishments.

There is plenty of work to attach in the more attendant educational adept fields. Reading books plus looking on line for job availability, computer networking& information technology, nursing medical assisting, dental/hygienists; seem to be the main job advertisements for authorization of future workers of the U.S. With the development of the electric or hybrid car, modern technologies have appropriated openings in alternate fields of work. Anyone across the nation can affirm with accuracy that with new inventions another job is activated. Although it appears the abundance of future jobs advertised should be in the computer or medical technical fields. Students today have to take dynamic advantage of an ample authentic college education in order to ameliorate to thrive or survive in this modern apprehensive adapt economy! Students have to achieve to abandon their old ways altogether adding affirmative affluent academically adventurous advice! Please adore the aptness of the allegories of these intellectual aphorisms!

The state of the economy used to be open allowing any aspiring assorted allocated ambitions! Our U.S. government has availed to abort the attraction of low income jobs, giving innumerable appreciable jobs to poor countries by accident? I've heard that our government accommodated to allow tax breaks to absentee companies to hire work here in the states, but instead these companies take the money for the adaptation of business in some other country? Don't be afraid we can assume the abstraction or abstention of these jobs guarantees the aperture of most jobs in the U.S. await skilled people that must have academicals of superior intelligence.

The government has anything but approved to attract the arrangement to set aside astonishing amounts of work to countries that pay awful wages. Even with alienating suspicion to available jobs, workers shouldn't run amuck. The U.S. made this deal so there is no aroused admonished amnesty recall to ask for the arcades of these jobs? This adamant action guarantees to make sure people of the U.S. have acute overall educational backgrounds before they can align alliance with assignment in the apron array of open jobs around the country. This proves the U.S. government is advisable to adjustments for rich smart people or the people of other countries! Of course U.S. unemployment rates attest artistically atrocious attentive arrogance?

It used to be, we the people of America when conversation of our agency of the national economy announcement came up. Right now it is as artificial articulation, when people want to say this government is, for the people by the people. Those artful words should be altered to government, for the rich by the rich. In God to wit we trust; all others must pay cash!

The government absolves themselves from being the alluring agents of abusive behavior to the acts of indigent people! How can we accentuate its government's fault when they conclude admittedly that they haven't been accompanying administrators in the angle of poor people's affairs anyway? The government has to abstain from denying the responsibility for the indigent's copious academic awestricken awareness! It doesn't take someone that has finished high school, anthropology or abstract analytical observation that this government allowed people to amazingly remain uneducated or miss-educated. Go out to be assaulted or witness who is being arrested; nine out of ten times the accused aggressor will be someone that in actuality, lacks education! Anywhere that there is one assailant I am sure he has one armed accomplice addict acting like the lookout standing on alert. I know I have been ambushed more than once!

When the Senate and House of Representatives were asked to assemble abolishing involuntary servitude in 1866, "Civil Rights Act", they were abashed addressing very little to administer the advocating of equal rights before adjournment! This absolutely amounted to advisory ambiguous adulterated abortive abnegation! It did very little to abridge the abyss with white people's adversary abrasive abrasion abomination of the black race. What equal rights?

The indigent black families were adaptable to farming acres of farm land, but very little else except singing or dancing while praying or working. The assimilation aggregation genesis of the genius of the black race hadn't arrived yet! The abased black's were always good-natured, conditionally akin to the alignment with agrarian attentions mostly hard acrobatic agricultural activity. The white man with their large plantations amused themselves hiring most of his black "free slaves" back with the allurement of free food, plus shelter. They made airtight adhesive agreements among "free slaves" again to adhere to the advocacy of their appetite for their addiction avarice of temporary great allowable plantation ownership. The "free slaves" plus their ancestors were allured to work for the food they ate plus their shelter. There were very little job alterations not any affections, adorations, money or the anticipation of announcing education.

This accusation would accord absurdity uneducated accompaniment for the "free slaves" to get accustom with! The abating black families were very ardent spiritual workers, mostly working for the LORD, enjoying their amazement aftermath of their assured "freedom". They were unaware of what the appendage of the arteries of the annotation of early enrichment of schools or education acumens can do to improve the advancements for the quality fulfillment of aright comfortable life of leisure! They were "free" to live arid artless lives from afar askance!

The "free slaves" had good healthy attitudes toward the aid of the aspect approaching agriculture works of their abusing white plantation owners. The aggregate group of "free slaves" was aloft being agriculturalist while looking toward their bosses for advisement. They arbitrarily agreed with the plantation owners without being adversaries not having arguments or altercations never wanting to attack their white bosses in anger. They were anchored maturing attributable to their amicable self accelerated opinions of this acquitted amiable life of announced "freedom"!

This would acquaint air tight accommodating conservation of energy, of the first degree, for the amusement of the acrid rich plantation owners against the comforts of their "free slaves". Rich, lazy ageing white farm owners were apathetic toward the answer to affix the abolition of educating his abase black farm hands; most weren't for antislavery or abolitionist?

What the hell the slaves were "free", what ass needs to adjust for more?! If his able-bodied workers were acceptable acquitting to work admirably from dawn till dusk tilling all the acreage of ground without being antagonistic that was the only agonizing accommodations needed! People don't have to activate intelligently to afflict the anguish amoral agility actions of the anatomy of continuous manual labor. To keep his black audience animated physically healthy would do very little to affect with the abetting astounding atmospheric intellectual endowments. Most plantation owners didn't have absorbed relative allowed ancestral airing affinities aligned.

This agenda of old fashioned government's absence let this abated educational process go abiding for approximately 100yrs. Adduce the math,(1866-1963-67). This assures our government should be ahead to announce alarmingly, for the rich by the rich. Conservatively speaking, that means most indigent's 40yrs of age or their adjacent ancestry have antipathy for the allotted proper education to be averring advisers in teaching their children anything? If people can't say the alphabet or convey basic intellect enough to being assistants in teaching of their children; well how intelligent will their children be? To asseverate the old adage here would be the apple doesn't fall far from the tree. Riches beget riches, poorness begets poorness, plus intellect begets intellect! It has only been since 1954, when the education avenue being aloof, abruptly finally assembled to be allied acquainting the allusion of awe of equal opportunity for equal rights to equal education. Which shall be our civil straight aim to adjudge its development?

The area of education was such annoying anonymous aching antisocial apocryphal the absent-minded arrogant government should have been alarmed? Treat people like animals, then what aberration should they amiss? This is one analysis of abject analogy aftereffects! Heck in 1967 the affray atrocities of the racial riots aggression annoyance was arguably the way to arouse the U.S. to start over. This was the agitation antidotes to avow this most absently abstruse aging government finally to acknowledge black people were really biped anthropoids or people just like white people? Where is the artisan attorney to appeal for allotting equal rights to upper education? We need one angel lawyer to use angelic powers to adjure education to astir anew.

Where is that one affectionate amorous analyst author that could give some analgesic antidote understanding why education was amputated or asphyxiated from black people's lives? It will take the application of 100 more years of allotted all-around education for us to be equal? The plantation owners, plus the aboriginal governmental employees should be accosted by one of those ten robbers that were aforementioned angrily awhile ago! "Freedom" from this antiquarian government's alleged stagnant counterfeit abnormality uneducated ancient atrophied abhorrence, is what's needed. That first 100yrs of artifice "freedom" the "free black slaves" were gave, was undeniably above accepting abominable abhor abuse! Reparations of the auricle needed now?

We can applaud this antiquated government for finally being the ablaze awakened announcer to accelerate congenial education allowance for people of every race. They were accepted in awarding conclusive animating attendance for alternatively being the amplifier in the aegis to help poor people's animation education, but to no avail. The augmentation avocation of dealing with the indigent's educational apprizing improvement would be anomalous! This ape government avidly applied these poor people with alms with applicable approbations never analyzes the amplitude in which money alters the apprehension of poor people? The government has finally started acceding to try avenging for years of attired aggravated asinine appropriations.

The government's afterthought has finally assigned alternate education in accordance so people can take additive educational classes to ascent their mental attiring. It would be nice to admire the great activation administration agreeable abutment allegiance, from the government to educate the poor people. The government can't apologize or have any alibis for the avowed misrepresentation of the abandoned anchorites of the U.S. The government doesn't want to assume responsibility for allegation animosities of the indigent's lack of education, abracadabra?

It is about too late for the amplification of the poorest ones abasement to approach the amenities of well to do's! What equal education can be received by alas, poor people, ah? The smart get richer, the rich get smarter, they can afford to! Most of us just forget about more school altogether alienated by the accelerating cost of education. It would be wonderful if this poor abstracted government could ascribe adjoining attainable assiduous affordable attributes?

It would be absurd if our arrant government was apologetic to the amity acceleration academic abilities of abnormal groups of indigent people. Whatever amount of education people could absorb, would apt to still be awry, too little too late, to be able to catch up with the rest of society. The government's all-out access to analyze the annals of poor people wasn't hidden or alien. What apparent ungodly governmental animosity caused us alluding educational aversion? With the proper ascendancy axes from government we can assure everyone adequate education.

We could argue that authorities were asleep or absent instead of being the artificers that aught ought to have fixed the abysmal horrific asperities that ail the indigent neighborhoods. Government should Americanize to awaken arbitrator ascendants avowed to be appertain agent accountants apace the audits of correcting the ailments amidst these neighborhoods. If our apex government afterward made amends to take accrued abridgment to annihilate or accomplish the about-face on ailing conditions that abound in poor neighborhoods, then we have absolute government alive, for the people by the people, not for the rich by the rich! The abodes some people abide within have always had the appearance of shacks with ugly eyesore blight that is not attractive. The askew crime rate has to be attenuated asunder so people can walk the streets without being abducted. With the authenticity of appending authorship of governmental auspices the annulment of unfit decay could be allayed alight to make this neighborly artery arc all right.

The assessment that the assessor assembling happens to be the auditors appraisal approximation that has lower tax rates compared to their suburban neighbors. The appearance of the home proves it has accordingly been taxed lower than their suburban neighbors, which is abreast of accidental illiteracy! The tax base for the educational apparatus is abasing in these neighborhoods; therefore students receive less money for their education. The government can avouch the active educational atmosphere has much less content with lower average financial funding attached per student. The indigent's annual tax base is so low; with this audit they have the same awfully old textbooks that their parents had? This educational asylum is bad acrimony!

Therefore, our government is adverse awkwardly adrift making the arrangements accounting for abundant higher education in their amateurish way? The government will forever be in the arrears with apologies helping along the arena of poor people in the U.S. Most rich aristocratic people of the U.S. have advanced apathy toward not wanting to ally with appeasing the qualms or accessories of poor peoples apparently appalling anxious apparition anxieties.

Women with much ado have only annexed the appointment to arbitrate alpha equal rights for 45yrs. It's been quite the athletic uphill battle which is closer to be astutely assembled then one can imagine! It's taking arbitration or the art to apply attrition with undying antagonism to eventually ascribing equal rights! It took assuring assumption of agitating force for women to appreciating pursuing affiliated to conclusively arresting acme equal rights. For sometime they had ably artfully been abused doing the same work at almost half the pay of men? Equal pay now is assiduously arranged assimilating that some woman might be adroit to demand the same pay! The aroused arrangement for equal pay is attenuating the pay gap ascribed between the sexes. Attributing factors to assembling associated attuned pay to become alighting now affords to exist. It will just take time for the alienation to the alias of men or women to finally awake to be audibly aboveboard the assimilated group of everyday associating aura of working people?

The alleviation or the separation from the aggravation of the old workforce certifies accentuating the accessibility of the adhesion of actors plus actresses, men plus women that have the authority to keep the actuation of this economy afloat. Allocating the accrual of the affiliation of everyone being avowal in the alignments of the work force ambitiously keeps the advertising; help wanted. The for hire sign used to be avowedly men wanted or maybe women needed, blacks please do not apply! Aladdin doesn't have to rub his magic lamp plus Ali Baba doesn't have to say "open sesame" to open the job market for women, blacks or legal alien's in the future awe-struck annexation of the workforce. This awaking of society needed alleviating the apprehensive aching accentuations that woman or blacks weren't qualified to achieving the same work for the same rate of pay! The accounting affably for future society is ascertainable to be mixed wit glee.

People can begin acknowledging this authenticated new abutting workforce isn't some affixed afoul anachronism. The ached afternoon conclusive aggressiveness adventuresome attitude of women or blacks was needed to improve society abundantly! These lay all-star efforts affiliating to adjusting abusive hiring's corrected the awkwardness in this administrative society? It would be wrong accusing that the absorbent of women plus blacks to the workforce caused the allocations of workers allergies or abate quality. This is especially true when Caucasian males authorizes the accredited workforce with women or blacks to be adjacently allies in working for the U.S.A. Black women will soon be advisable to aerate their absolved abided presents in the accruing workforce. The U.S.A. has said its last adieu to apologizing for discrimination. The lull adducing that the affidavit of the working males autographs the admitting of women or blacks can be equals in the workforce; not corrosively adulterating that was the addictive afoot idea!

When admiring the alleging advent affair of the annulling of discrimination one has to be appeased with the afterglow of complete harmonious humanity. For women plus African Americans their amalgamating force to receive auditions allying within the workforce appeared propelled with the adornment of God or Allah! In the beginning the alamode or fashions of their daily lives wasn't for the appeasement of the alabaster male's livelihoods. Anglo-American poor males didn't want women or blacks in the workforce. With the airily use of the good applications of authorizing women to work during WWII proved the appareling woman was anatomical fit for annexations of the appliance of advanced factory working afterwards. It's not addled alienation!

The black Tuskegee Airman proved his actuations for good work within this aerated society with their aeronautic aide flying airplanes in the WWII! They had some aces during the aerial aviations or air strikes flying in WWII! The Air Corps of Tuskegee Institute in Alabama trained "The Redtails" to be exceptional agents in aeronautical aviation operations of war! They were aviator guides for air force bomber planes. With the aircraft they protected admiringly to fly to new altitudes with their altimeters in air raids. With these allegorical operations the blacks acquit their alacrity wasn't too aimlessly or contagiously be allergic to working agog with white males. Their immediate analogies showed this great acclimatized workforce was indeed alterable without acquisitive apologies. Adjoining the work force women or blacks accorded to be equals!

Men shouldn't be agitated for annihilating the old workforce to absolving the new workforce, all-American people! The airy agreeing to annul the adversities of the alibi to axe discrimination helps complete the applicability to Americanisms correcting the amorphous of the U.S. working citizens. The country took alright shape deleting this abuses which didn't cause the adulterations of the workforce in no shape or form. One could admirer with adoration the anti-climax analyzing of the amalgamations of the nation's new aligning august workforce improving annually. The annulled discrimination helps affability aglow in people in this working society.

It has been abhorrently accursed the way women were looked down upon! Men will finally have to abash the abjuration that they should be abdicating the arbitrated equal rights for women? Nowadays women supply 60% of the authenticating work force. Only time will tell if men will absolutely consider that the ablest women can be their 100% equals? The ABC's of the architectural balancing arithmetic for the pay scales for different companies can never be totally analyzed without the intelligence of the ghost of Archimedes or other superior godly ordained apostle committed genius mathematician. Intelligent women can be assured that they shouldn't be steadily arguing for their being shorted on pay. Women can assertively be their own aspirant assistant in their averred qualified position of articulating the assemblies of the ascription for the arising jobs of their choice. The asseveration of working women has arisen to be equal to men!

The U.S. government can't become a dictator or arbiter to annotate the abjuring architecture to apprehend the aorta aqueduct pay rates of people. The private sector is off limits for government to be abroad arousing to have peoples pay availability averaging or totally attend balancing pay anatomically. The pay might throw some women aback to be abruptly wrong; they work in the arbor of the archway of their own arbitrary accomplishing pay rates. The aborigine's anterior company managers archly set pay scales suitable to themselves which never appreciated the astuteness of women! Their never can accurately be assailable ideas put to business set in its austerity album of the permanent old arcade foundation of years in the working order of things?

The assigned augury abasing of women is just one of the annoying accidents or odd autopsies of the evolution of acclimatizing society to accelerate to reach its final artifact essence! Women continue to be aspired arduously fighting for equal rights to abridging the gape to finally receive the awed axis equal pay that's attributed to men. With straight arrow arithmetical figures there can't be arranging set pay for all jobs? The armful of armchair armaments to protect the pay scale is aristocratically set. No one can fight the austerely authoritatively atrociously affixing armature of nature? What will be, will be, that is the atom of the total awing amnesia of reality.

Only time will tell what abilities of the abnormalities for the magical abductors of this arbitrating antitrust will do to attenuate the approximated pay differentials? The very idea to assimilate equal pay rates is totally beyond the realities of the approximating arms of the very assuming architect for complementing society. It would take the anthology work of the alchemist to use alchemy to quench the appetites or argument to the assertion of equal pay for everyone. There should be the asterisk next to the set up, men vs. women, of the full abdicate associating people in this original acclimated newer society. Without the advice of Aristotle or attendances from some other great thinker's philosophical ideas the agonized pay adjunct appendix absents for equal pay will have to be avoided or not answerable! Working shouldn't addle our activities!

Women ardently argued that their pay appropriately be averaged with that of armfuls of working men! People or the abutting astronauts of this world have to use their astronomy or astrology to reconfigure their appreciation to keep alighted for attenuated conversation for aye allusive equal pay. There is no sense fighting what is affecting the deficient abysmally idea's of the cast to the authenticity of concurrent reality? The quaint augur armoring assimilation of good education for people will be the authorized advising appropriating audition arterial to anvil the audibility to assuredly have hammered equality into society! Not too much affection has been used for abridges of affected equal pay that may have to be additionally administered to workers.

Women plus black people alike had to fight away through great aggrieving adversity to access their rights to work along-side white males instead of amply alone. It took incredible admiration to fight for rights that should have already been axioms. Women had to appeal to arrange the government to finally get proper admission augment arrival of considerable equal pay with men, without too much anarchy from the avid manly citizens. Women finally have authority to acclaim them additionally accountable accumulating applicable attainments.

Women plus black people can authorize to appoint assimilative assertive austere admissible awakening attuning. The U.S. has black mayors in every major city, plus we now have, Mr. President Barrack Obama, our first black president. The addition of women in the work force is not anarchic but quit analogous with men. Women continue to add apportioned constituencies in plenty of local accessible governmental offices! The additions of women in the work force can only help with its alit amelioration. These accolades or accredits prove that good ammunition for abrogating discrimination is for the essential accession of the whole artistry assortment of the human race. The antecedent antics affecting the articles of discouraging most major discrimination were patriotic harmony atop altruistically axiomatic anomaly avalanche.

"I have a dream we shall over-come", what the honorable, Dr. Martian Luther King asserted, on August 28th, 1963, is what's astoundingly actively accurately advancing now aha, amen. It took some absorbing averse times but discrimination is falling apart, totally going down, like some great ambidextrous anointed prize fighter. The ambled ameliorating of society truly amenably helps people coexist. The advancement of this aggressive adventure will continue until this aged agony is amended altogether amongst altruism. In the near future "we will over-come", this aristocracy of the astronomical astute audacious Anglo-Saxon authoritative Americanism!

The rich get richer, the poor get poorer. Someday with authenticated acquiescence ardor; the poor will arise to become the agitator to amalgamate new altitude awards with great awesome auxiliary. Bravely, not feeling the guilt from past aspersions or ashamed from being aware they once were the human antithesis.

It will take destiny or assent assiduities that the associations of the poor amass riches from their great abasements to finally attain ascertain articulated adherent atonements. The poor will get richer awaiting their agile adjustable adherence aggrandizing apexes! The rich people are not better than the poor albeit, the rich will try to alienate the poor, attempting to antagonize them with artistic argumentative acrimonious slanderous remarks.

Being poor aren't some afflictions of life to get accustomed to. Without apology amenable appreciative persistent assemblage of scholarly study, "I have a dream we shall over-come", to assail amendments with assuring what's greater than this ascetic American life has to offer. It will take almighty relentless amazing audacity without going astray, plus the proper ambitious atoning assistance from associated education to assess assets to aspire in this vast economical world. The ambling ambassadors of the poor without ambiguities well sense the ambrosia archives of great undeniable knowledge helping them to ambush the rich intellectually!

The poor will auspiciously be the archetype to arm their minds with the Argus of ascertained positive thinking arousing the arsenal of the aroma of the stinking rich to aptly reach complete annotated acquiescing. The arising army of the poor will be armored with the axial of humanly wise proportional prodigious aromatic educational predominate arch; the argosy of the rich will have to give up to the great Ares of the poor! With this abbreviating abler abdication of the gape that's, from rich to poor, people will finally be aboard becoming equal to atrophying monetary ambiguity abeyance forever. Let's say adios aloud to amend anguished old aggravating discrimination! Remember, the poor with orderly alternating appointive education can aim to alleviate the rich of their biggest burden, money. With assuaging acknowledgment these rich people include 90% of government officials that have arduous archaic applied aptitude anyhow?

Zoo Daze

My whole family gets together at least twice a year to have a barbecue or basket picnic at the Detroit Zoological Park. I'm the boss of the barrel of fun that we have every one of our zoo days! I try my best to beautify our day and become the main backer of our trip to the zoo. Barring any lousy weather the backlog of things needed for bagging our one day trip is taken care of beforehand. I have the background and know how to take care of all the bulkiest things that we need brought together on behalf of our zoo trip. Buying things a couple days ahead of time blots out the rushing to get over the huge barricade of items that we have to build up for our beauteous day at the zoo. Once I have begun bundling things together the bedlam of the bombardment of the biggest bulkier things that have to get done won't get brutal!

My sister Sally bakes the cookies or brownies the night before we go. Having her bake saves going to the bakery and spending money. I'm a frugal shopper so the kids help me pack a picnic bag with everything we might need. I take my mustard, ketchup; a couple loafs of bread for butcher bologna and cheese sandwiches, chips, fruits, and vegetables. Sometimes we have hot dogs, burgers and buns. We have a cooler on wheels full of ice, bottles of pop, water, beer any beverage or brew we need to drink for our budding zoo day. We go bananas for the trip!

I always bathe then, bundle up with baggiest blazer in the morning and take my most bearable little walk that gets me started for a wonderful day at the zoo. The mornings in May are cool and brisk. Picking the balmiest (70's) degree day for our zoo day is a bonus for our family's biological bout. I have to borrow my friend's mini bus that has beneficial space for all our trusty supplies and the kids. We had 14 seats of the vehicle filled to the brim for our benignly zoo trip

We bustle all our belongings together that will benefit our zoo day. I take my first aid kit with everything including, bandages. I even take binoculars which is no bother in bracing our boundless day of fun. I never want to leave anything behind. I'm not a beginner and I couldn't boast of our good times if the kids got bummed out if I botched our zoo day! I would bend over backwards to by-pass the blur of things that I would have to bewail if they weren't taken care of ahead of time. The kids bring balloons, balls, bubblegum, candy, dolls and our little red wagon. I stay within my budget and buy everyone a brunch buffet to start our day with a bang. This meal is a barometer for us to begin our biannual adventure to see how everyone is feeling. The meal makes sure the kids don't badger me about eating. With the discounts I'm not breaking myself.

I bought my grandfather pass that is beneficiary to us for entrance to the park for less than a hundred dollar bill. Basically it is a discount pass that is good for a year. It allows two adults and all my beggar kids 12 years or younger that are with me to get in the zoo for free. I won't get burnt or empty my billfold paying too much admission! I almost feel like a burglar that is bilking them on the price. I can bet a trip to the zoo won't bankrupt me. I can't go every day; it is too much walking for my bungled old body! Why act a brooder when I can just go whenever?

The entrance into the zoo is a giant bottle-neck that takes borderline boldness to not try bolting through the people to procure entrance into the park. I'm not a bungler so I wanted to avoid the black list or banishment for busting in. This would be barbarous so we wait with the other people. Anyone can see me setting on the bench waiting to get in. Sometimes I read the bulletin boards just biding my time with the other bystanders. I was in a bloc of 14 people this year at the zoo. Ten got in for free. It is fine to act frugal and accept this brand-new deal while banding together to have a barreled day of fun without any backslidings from the babied kids.

When I was healthy I run three miles to work and home again every day. The day I was 35yrs old then saw and heard the barking of 12 dogs, was the last time I ran to work! If I hadn't ran so fast the dogs would have had a good breakfast? About 22 years ago I broke my hip. I'm lucky that I'm not bedridden now, the doctor told me that 99 out of 100 die from the type of accident that I had! My bungling hip breakage was caused from going 65 miles an hour to 0 in twenty feet! Now I'm unable to walking more than a eighth of a mile! The breaking was so bad; the kids bicker with me over our rental buggy, barrow, or wheelchair we use to glide around the exciting park.

After walking a while I have to take a breather, plus the kids are boundlessly lazy, those are bygone days for me to walk all day! I ride in the wheelchair because my old legs can't take it. The buffoon kids will bounce or bump me out of the wheelchair and break my bifocals or my brittle bald head if I'm not careful of their playful banter that they bombard me with. They have bounced me off the wheelchair with the bumpiest of breakneck rides on the by-path already! They like barreling or batting me around the bricklaying of the sidewalks in the park with the wheelchair and sometimes hit the upheaval cracks in the brickwork. Their buffoonery is okay as long as it doesn't end up backfiring to hurt someone that's falling on the brick walkway!

There isn't a blueprint for taking our trip to the zoo. I noticed for years that families and busses of school kids dress with the brightness of the same color shirts, blouses, bloomers, breeches, bonnets, anything to help find your friends and family! We all were bound in beige last year to blend together. I take a bundle of people to bustle around the zoo never worried about bumpy financial barriers that I can't handle. I take care of business like a businessman should without any burden in the world besides what taking care of a bountiful of people has to contend with. Once we are all in the zoo our blissful blessed binding biology blossoms.

When we first walk in, we saw a brood of sparrows, peacocks everywhere, blue jays, blackbirds and just about any bevies of bird a person can name. The first home built for animals we saw was a huge aviary that has thousands of butterflies in a beautiful bushy botanical garden, planted with a botanist expertise within its lovely brick-work walls. This is quite a breath-taking site to behold which instantaneously gives one a broadened burst of wonderful energy for a day.

I had trouble last year a couple of times. One problem I'll talk about later and the other was the kids wanting to behave in their own way all the time! The younger babies, 5-8 yrs old, were always badgering me. They almost wanted to backhand me for not letting them pet the animals! The lovely peacocks walked up to us bending their heads up so we could put food in their beaks. Sometimes the kids bawled and cried like banshees after I blurted out that the zoo animals might bite! None of us ever got hurt while we were bombing around the zoo all day!

When we got close to the prairie dogs the bursting excitement really began. It was fun going past the bulwark or buttress of the walls and getting in the middle of their habitat. We like getting underground banging on the glass watching the bushiest prairie dogs as they busied to burrow their holes in the banks of sand. The only buffer we had around us was a submerged glass and cement bunker. The kids were excited getting so close to these bushier little animals they seem to bubble with excitement and blare out babbles when they talked! Just name an animal and the Detroit Zoological Park, probably has them! We were able to see farm animals, bighorn sheep, beavers, badgers, bunnies, burros, bison, buffalo, bears and even baboons.

They have little ponds and brooks for the amphibians and fish. There is a little bridge that we cross and bide our time feeding the fish. We saw plenty of reptile's bull-frogs, boa-constrictors almost every frog and snake imaginable within their own sanctuaries with glass aquariums from top to bottom! The kids and adults briefly have a truly wonderful educational experience with a day at the zoo. The children want my attention and beckon me to see this and that all the time. I have a map so we can see everything and I can relieve my bloated bladder.

There are little shower basins all over the park that allow everyone to cool off if they want. The kids quite often are behaving wildly not caring about listening to anything anyone says; we are there to have fun anyway. I feel bravely blameless with my day at the zoo. I actually feel like I'm in the beauty of a different world! I can't budge away from these special busiest zoo days. Never is there a time that I buckle under pressure for all the bustling of things we have to get together for our nice day! This all proves a balmy day in May is a perfect bulls-eye for our family's breathless barefoot play in the very interesting beguiled Detroit Zoological Park!

One of our favorite spots when we enter the zoo is a barnyard with bales of hay lying in a bin baled for the animals bedding. We also saw a bushel of oats to feed the well bred animals. The large barn has a horse, cows, donkeys, goats, and boar hogs as the main beast and peacocks that go everywhere. I did have a boyhood dream a bit of farming when I was young! A trip to the zoo almost makes dreams of baling hay come true. We can hear the bellows of the bull, the bray of a donkey and the squeal of the pigs. The kids act so babyish while listening to the animals bleating loud and clear. It's bewitching to browse thru these backstage godly zoo byproducts!

A few years ago I had lost my bearings at the zoo before I knew what happened! My sister lost her brooch and back-tracked to find it. I laid a blanket out to relax in the sun and passed out instead. Boy it was a bonfire nice hot breezy beguiling day at the zoo, maybe about (80) degrees! For some reason I made a blunder by staying away from my doctor to long. It was a bizarre bittersweet day when my head got bleary and I passed out. When I made a belated visit to the doctor the next day to find out my blood pressure was too high it probably saved my life! I found out that I had hypertension which the doctor gave me medicine to blot it out putting the blear beneath me! I had been baffled at different times by getting dizzy and losing my balance. Now I can boldly say the bewilderment of hypertension had bamboozled me for one year. Most zoo daze develops the betterment of the whole beautiful blooming bothersome bouncing bunch.

It's befuddling to me that my brother and brother-in-law don't ever want to go to the zoo. They claim that it is beyond the boundaries that they can walk and they are afraid of blisters! I even told them that I would pay their way in! That just proves they are lazy. There is not any comparison between the cost and breadth of the accumulation of our busier exciting times. I consider a trip to the zoo as a banner bargain. When I go to the bank and get some money from the banker, I never can get more bangs for the buck! My old bedraggled self will never bemoan a wonderful zoo trip that is for the beneficence of us all, an excellent bondage to the whole family?

I walk the bricks until I'm on the brink of a breakdown. My legs, backbone or fat bellied self won't allow me to over exert myself! I'm biped like most people of the world. I would blush in shame if someone wanted my bulky bulged body to walk more than a half hour, no way would I make it! What a boastful boyish kind of guy I was until the car accident makes it hard to walk. I used to sometimes brag about my brazen athletic abilities. Never one to boasting too much, at 5-8, I could almost dunk a basketball, bat a baseball, made a one-man triple play in softball, kick a soccer ball, bowl a 200 game, run table in billiards. I also set 6 records in track. Running the fastest in the army, I run 2 miles, ate breakfast, then went to the barracks for a long nap! Now the basis for my burdensome butt to get fat is my inabilities too exercise my broken-down physique, nothing to brood about! I still like bragging about my old nickname I braced, Jumping Jack Flxxx!

Learning is a breeze when a person is younger! For this godly reason I wish my education could have bewitched the way I'm trying to type this book? I type in such a bestirring bestrewed way I hope this story is a brightly bombastic brilliancy to some readers. This is the only time that I would need a bib, to wipe besmearing tears from my bloodshot eyes blamed on my brassy inabilities to type right! I'm never a braggart about my brainy bookkeeping or boring begrudged typing abilities! I'm a bookish type of a guy reading nowadays; indecently bookworm booby is now my new acquired nickname! Anyhow I'll forget my bravos from my pecker typing and will get breezing toward the main story with the brainiest swiftness that one can have bourn. I always broadcasted that I was a proud Beecher Buccaneer, physically not so much mentally?

Anyone that looks at me now believes that my blubber belly belongs to a young lady that is about to be a mother in four months, the blob or blimp! The trip to the zoo is badly needed exercise for me plus a balanced educational ordeal for all my believing behooving fine family members. We all are bent banking on the next wonderful befalling bonuses for our next visit to the zoo. My birthday May 21st is about the time we hit the blacktop for our first visit to the zoo with the end of August our last. The zoo visits are a brief broad branch brilliant building block.

My relatives can't say that I'm the benighted black-sheep of the family! We will go bundled together again next year to boost the balminess befitting of our family buoyancy! A family that plays together stays buoyant together. It always brightens the kid's day to hear grand—pa-pa or Uncle Jack broadcast, it is zoo time today! My son and daughter both have a chance for romance with their spouses when I baby-set all the kids for our zoo day. Sometimes my kids go to the zoo only, they say that their too old (40) and need a babysitter for the day! It's always a blast when we visit the zoo with little boohooing brawling actions or backtalk brickbat from the brats. It's a breach of contract if I don't pick a bright balmier day in May to beguile a zoo day.

The other problem I had was a bigger built brutish blond-haired guy tried attacking me last year! He must have drunk to much brandy or just left the bar with a good belching buzz on. It upset us badly when my blameworthy 6yr old nephew busily bumped the bumper of his car accidentally with our little plastic red wagon. I was in shock trying to talk breezily to this huge, crazy uncontrollable bone breaker of a masculine guy! I bade him to hurry begetting to go!

He behaved like a boxer that had bats in the belfry! If he went ballistic on me he would begrime our wonderful zoo day! He acted like some brainless brawny busybody barbarian wanting to bury me below the ground. Wow, I wasn't blind this beefiest bull of a battler guy could bludgeon me with one bloodcurdling barbaric blow! I wasn't ready for a burial and the bullies talk or barbed voice was mostly baseless bunk anyway. He had the brassiest bad-temper and was probably someone's bodyguard? As I listened to his sad brokenhearted based bellicose conversation in a benumbed way I assumed that he belonged to a health club somewhere to boot?

The bulk of him was bulging with burley muscles, his biceps were huge. I had to make sure his bullying bid to belt or batter me backfired on him! I was blest to hold him at bay and use the benefaction of my brave brain with balancing attrition to beget mind over matter to control this beefier mean blood-thirsty bodybuilder man beater! There was no way that I wanted to balk or buckling my chance to stop his bidding barbarity in a non-violent fashion! This brute could do bodily harm and make me bleed if he batted me on this banned battlefield. I stood my ground with bated breath!

It seemed like a blackout of fear was near as I bashfully faced the bigness of this well bodied boisterous guy. I could have blazed a beeline into my vehicle, my future looked bleak. Someway I had to get bustling to bolster the bravado to beg for his mercy, not go blank and betray my kids! For sure anyone would beware of his blatant base beliefs to protect and defend their beloved children. I had to bare the brass facts to brace myself and brandish the bravery to stand up to this bullies actions for binding brotherly love instead of bawdy battling barbarism? It was hard to breathe; I was turning blue in fear from the barrage of the biased brunt brash bigot brutality this bowlegged backwoodsman looking bumpkin of a guy was besieging upon us!

It seemed like a lifelong ordeal but I continually bustled budging him in a blunt bland way to belittle his bewildered bitter blasphemy he belligerently besieged upon us, with his very deep bass voice! I was broad-minded and with intense brevities talked kindly to him while the bionic-beast of a guy begrudgingly raised his brow above his big beady eyes talking to me from within his breast in a befogging berserk blusterous voice. Getting busy with my attractive bastion attrition brilliance I befriended him. This was one time my face wouldn't get bashed, bruised or battered! This bodybuilding guy could have made me black-eyed or black-and-blue on this very sacred battleground! Using ones brains begets proportionate power once in a while, I think?

My benign benevolent brevity ways bestowed a batch of bilateral condolences amongst two befuddled guys and eventually we were buddies without bloodshed! To give Bob twenty bucks for the scratch on his car did help cure his bestial manners and my baffling bashfulness! Brotherhood was found with a beam of hope to boldly beseech bask beneficent benevolence.

That was one of our bogus blemished zoo daze! Fighting is something that doesn't bode well with my borne loving personality. I was a very lucky benefactor to bribe or bluff him into a gentle bloodless submission! Of course I'll never get belligerent with anyone. My belief is that it is best to never berate anyone, it is better to offer your blessings then to offer a good bloodied booty beaten! It's amazing that my convincing conclusive bid barely beat this basic beastly battle! It behooves me to always befit beholden before beginning begrudged behavior!

(I-PENTAMENT)

WORLD PEACE

I stands independently a word familiarized by egotistical people in love with themselves. The ingredient for this love is infinite, the kind of love we should share with all humanity. Procurement of inter-continental love and peace would instantly be what most governments want. Spreading love and peace instantaneously inhibits people's ability to live unconditionally of their own free will. Most people of different governments feel insecure with this intake of superficial involuntary servitude of another country! We find world peace by implanting international intervention incredibly impossible.

For world peace governments should be able to impart an incantation by a worldly indefatigable indefinable inceptor, for all governments to use dealing with the exaltation of impervious stately affairs. What an intuitive fanciful thought, to have a worldly tenet or constitution to have an internationalized intoxicating invocation interview interchange. Our worldly intercourse would be intensely institutional without any intermission!

These plans are impractical not realistic enough; maybe we could start implying something almost real like, immediately instill interesting intricate interjections. Introduce interpretations immunize inept individuals. Illuminate impressive improvised indentured inventions. Ignite incalculable immaculate incorporeal idiosyncrasies. Individualize immeasurable invigorative invaluable ideas. Intuitively improve inaccurate impalpable investments. Insure information illustrative immersing imaginations.

To control world peace we should have incipient inculcating incontrovertible indivisible imperishable imperative indicators! These are just a few ways for improvising indeterminate considerations toward correcting worldly incidental incisive ideology inexhaustible indecencies. Let's forget all these great imperceptible fanciful incoherent inconsistent incompatible tribulation images and go back to where inevitable idolizing began!

Adam and Eve were told, Genesis-(2-17) "But of thee tree of knowledge of good and evil, thou shall not eat of it: for in the day thou eatest thereof thou shalt surely die." Later the serpent said, Genesis-(2-24)"Ye shall not surely die" When Adam took an incautious impertinent bite of the fruit; this was the first incriminating impeding malicious act to have infected or injure the ingratitude of humanity! The definition of war: MALICIOUS.

Intellectually insinuating, Adam and Eve initially started the immortalizing impious malevolent activities to impel the indignities of humanity. Without wars an ever more indecisive overabundance of people would subside on this earth? Wars effectually intrigued to provide God's emancipation for the injustice of the world's first sin. That initial sin inserted an infernal indebted inextinguishable indescribable insolvable incorrigible alpha war amongst God's people.

Disproportion sequential inference, had Adam and Eve not ate of the impure fruit from the tree of knowledge of good and evil, we would not know of war, we would not be knowledgeable, we would all be insensible idiots. The world would be over populated with an abundance of impractical immature moronic imbeciles! Adam and Eve had committed a sin officially injecting immutable incurable inescapable indissoluble impiety iniquity ill-will.

Obviously life and death are an impending ingrained part of humanity an inseparable infallible inflexible infused inscription. Nonsensical evolutionary inoculation of war irrelevantly proficiently impolitely propitiates implicit knowledge. World War I, (1914-1918), caused the deaths of an innumerable amount of people. No one really knows how many people died in this war? Inquiring historians with their investigations insist that about 10 million died impudently?

There was an interlude of about 20yrs when Germany in 1939 entered Poland; starting World War II (1939-1945).According to Hitler's imperialist idolatry instructions, Mein Kampf (1924), Germany had to integrate Russia's land. Germany invaded Russia (1941) and had Italy and Japan on their side. The Russian infrastructure and millions of Russians were totally destroyed from this invasion. The U.S. had already given billions of dollars to Great Britain and Russia toward an insufficiency of fighting the infidel German's. The U.S. incisively insisted they were impelled to stay out of the insanities or iniquities of the injuries of war, as the world turns.

On Dec.7th, 1941 Japan bombed Pearl Harbor which was a very insulting insolent intolerable inclement incident for the U.S. to inscribe. The impudent insertion of these bombs inspired the impulsion infuriating the inanimate U.S. to inconvenience the U.S. Pentagon to be inclined to impose the declaration of war on Japan. The U.S. had no interest and never intended to impair the insanity of war upon its people. The U.S. government insists that the only insurance to keep our freedom intact was to fight to imprint our rights instead of becoming an insufficiently inferiority or infirm incapacitate injured indentured servitudes to huge Japan, as the world turns!

The U.S. government had the ill impulse or instinct to imprison most of Japanese immigrants at this time. These abrupt incarcerations keep immunity from all real or insubstantial illusions of terrorism. The immodest ill-treatment was meant to immobilize any imaginary illicit terrorists thoughts the Japanese inmates might have had. If the Japanese were terrorists this great government could only imagine all the injuring damage that could be done inside the U.S.A. The intensity from the U.S. government to interact with the internment of Japanese during World War II invalidated any inward introductory intrusion of terrorism. I've tried to interpret why the government had to intend to intrude with the interceding intricacies of war, as the world turns.

The U.S. government made an impression toward the interception of war with the inclusion of insurmountable imaginative impunity to import industrializing intelligible instructed individualities. The imposition to invest into the inventory of war was one instance that gave insight to inspect or inquire about our infectious innovation infancy of our instrument of united industry! The introduction of U.S. factory workers inspiration was indispensable and saved American culture. Our identities and our very independence would have been insistently inoperative, taken by Japan, had Americans been inexpert or incommensurate at factory work during World War II! We all would have been part Japanese, Americanize, as the world turns!

There were approximately 25-35 million deaths during World War II, with some indications 5-10 million or more were citizens killed for their, religious views or beliefs, their race or for just taking up space! Being a kind hearted soul incapable talking about death and destruction, especially the genocide of any race, World War II finally ended. The inquisition of worldly records of birth and death were inapplicable irrecoverable inexact informally idle improperly ignored! With inconsiderable inaccuracies my inappropriate inconsequential innate math, there would be 2-3 billion more people, without these ill-gotten wars, as the world turns!

Now I'll try to infer an imbue illustration for the importance of the indifferent ill-fated indiscretions of the industrious indulgence of the life and death of the impasse of war. My father, a World War II veteran, bless his soul, produced the inception of 90 plus people on this earth. Being a veteran of the Vietnam War my inheritance has produced 10 plus people and so on, without interruption there will be infinities of birth and death. To be a little more informative and further illustrate my immovable imbibe, dad and myself caused the births of 100 people and counting. It might not impress anyone, but for two to produce one-hundred, 45 million would imply? Our babies will indubitably have babies, irrespectively by wedlock or illegitimately, even when we are gone, thank God for survival, as the world turns! Another infant was born today!

The most agile country with a magnificent immortal impassioned cultured mental disposition will indomitably win most wars. Darwinism inclinations include that the strong will imminently survive. With human beings this theories instant integral input intrinsically inordinately invariable. Human domination incubating impracticable imperfections adhere consistently to the improvement of the cultivated mind over matter. Albert Einstein on the U.S. government's side during World War II took the ingenuity to prove mind over matter! With his superior encephalon Mr. Einstein instituted instructive inventive ingenious intelligence being able to annihilate matter to infinitesimal molecules. This incontestably proves mind over matter! Most people on this earth find war intelligently intimately infamous inexorably irrational? Please excuse this implicating inelastic interaction euphemism-God does everything, as the world turns!

Third world inert indigent countries impatiently find sustenance through the U. S. government's inflow of instrumental distribution of provisional commodities. These inapt countries transparent infantile posterity would be illusive without U.S. governmental instigated inspirational extraordinary influx of implementations fundamental toward reviving rudimentary essential elements of survival. We could try imperfect invasive imponderable impenetrable indoctrination? These impoverished countries are interconnected improvidently with their imposing insignificant insufficient inappropriate ways. All foreign governments are considered instigating incoming intruders with a ludicrous insipid foreign policy, as the world turns!

The U.S. government's importation of their frivolous chauvinism juxtaposition causes the inertia of poor countries to increase initiative inducing indefinite impediments. They will fight indiscriminately for a government which will be indistinctly inconspicuous inefficient immaterial incomplete inequitable ineligible. Why should these inhospitable countries trust the U.S. when they are inure to not even trust each other? U.S. government inherently shares love and peace throughout the world. A large percentage of the world population doesn't want U. S. governments help purging their inborn inconsiderate impulsive inane indelicate imprudence.

The U.S. government helps protect the world from terrorism. Terrorists intermingle with normal everyday people; the iteration interspersion of terrorists makes them always look incognito, imaginary imitative indistinguishable invisible, insanely hard to find. Terrorist indiscreetly make infrequent indecent impeding incursions all over the globe without invitations. After finding the innermost inland inhabitable unprotected target, terrorist begin their never ending intimidating revengeful irritant acts to imperil the greatest damage! Inclusive identifying informalities indicate terrorist main intensions are to indiscriminately infiltrate isolated inhabitants innocence with incapacitated ill-bred infractions of totally inharmonious violence!

Terrorist's insurgent inexplicit incomprehensible insidious acts on innocent people irrelevant to the benefit of any one! Terrorists intentionally blow up dams, cars, planes, boats, buildings, even themselves for some intriguing invalid preposterous ungodly religious belief they incorrectly claim to be gloriously righteous? There has to be an instinctively inaugurating impounding of the great itinerant acts of terrorism to ordain the supreme incapacity to these acts!

It'll take incorruptible individualism to invent incapacities to the inner induction of the great intemperance infecting infiltration acts of the immensity of terrorism. I'd implore anyone to make an instinctive impromptu suggestion to impound the plentiful terrorist inconstant incendiary hurtful encumbrances! There has to be interposing intensification introducing iron-clad interceded isolation of the intermittently insensate injury acts of the inhumanity of terrorism. Someday with unrelenting solidarity the world might intervene with interdependence to interrupt with this impulsive irregular illegal illogical irresponsible irreverence's.

The TWIN-TOWERS epitomizes the identification of what has to be done to insulate the world from the insurrection of ignominious incivilities of the interminable irritation from inscrutable terrorism! With great respect and condolences to all that lost family and friends at the eruption of (9-11), please forgive my embarrassing inconvenient inability to talk about such sordid and base tragedy. This act was an inconceivable ignorant insensitive immoral incubus inhuman indignation! The U.S. government incomparably protected the world from irrepressible idiocy idolater terrorism. While protecting the world from intermittent terrorism the U.S. borders were found inexpedient! The inattentive inactions of the U.S. government caused irretrievable death and destruction of the homeland of the United States of America! The ineptly informality of these terrorist inflammations will never be forgotten! This act caused the U.S. government's injunction to intensify inauguration of impassable indestructible impregnability.

With supreme reverence terrorism interrupted after years of U.S. affirmative intermediary intuition inundating incentives compiling fraternal rectifications throughout the world. The U.S. started initializing influential impelling actions toward correcting coarse diverse interrelated inconsistencies of worldly affairs. Amazingly, the ignition inlet of U.S. government illustrious indemnities impersonate the works of a miraculous immaterialist conceptualist, a great inhabit overseer with entire populous subjects to total investigation. He who helps himself does not need any help at all, which should be the most imaginable admirable thought to cause sovereign indisputable intensive interchangeable internal incitement. This concept would imitate exactly what the U.S. government wants to begin inveigling or evolving. To control world peace the U.S. government's intrepidity must install instrumentality important intangible immense insulators! The U.S. government tenaciously protects the world from terrorism, third-world countries are protected by the U. S. intermediate interposition interlude invincible internship.

Inevitably something has to be inaugurated to idealistically extinguish or immure irresponsible intolerant inveterate indefensible terrorism itself! Innovations of superior strategies aimed at the impingement of terrorist impetus attacks are currently inundated ineffectually being enforced. The U.S. government sends its inexperienced troops or infantrymen all over the globe to protect the integrity of people from inroad terrorism. The ignorance of terrorisms injury can be initiated within the interiors of a substantial number of foreign countries. The U.S. government incessantly issue military installation investitures mandatory toward developing progressive prosperity dealing with terrorisms inexplicable inexpressible injurious idolatrous idealism.

The illimitable illustrating of the incongruous informalities of terrorism has to be inherently stopped. Nobody has the inkling to immuring the implicating impoliteness of the harmful infractions from terrorism! The inundations of the impolite inauspicious intimidations' of terrorism have to be corrected! Every generation will inherit the impatience of the always implicating inadvisable obscene terrorism! Any informant can interject that the means for totally incarcerating the incorrectly inclined acts of ingrate terrorist can't be found? We'll have to live without an idealistic form of peace and harmony, since the infection of terrorism has forever had independently inconvenienced insurability's to the imminence of a comfortable peaceful world!

World peace will never become a reality unless injudicious terrorism impatience absorbs an improbable complete irradiating annihilation of terrorisms incorrectly insatiable insane irritating interferences! The world's complicated complexion or complexity makes world peace an extremely irreparable irrevocable item. The infestation of terrorist indecorous intrigue will always infringe on worldly peace and harmony. All worldly actions and reactions have instinctive equilibrium to impact the infinitude incongruity balance of nature, as the world turns!

The earth happens to be a domain full of the intellectual dominate animal the ever irritable impressionable human being. All countries want to inform everyone that their idiomatic way must be the impeccable way to deal with the ever imposing human affairs? When one country goes broke they all irresistibly go broke which happens to be an impartial inalienable illness phenomenally conducive of an omnipresent executioner interfering with the initialing injection of the endorsement of worldly affairs! Who might this mighty invulnerable illumining intimidating infiltrating interracial omnipresent interposed executioner be, as the world turns?

For everyone on this earth this magical being of supreme knowledge invokes interim inducements of things to happen in a mystical hypnotically inviolable ineffable impetuous impersonal irrefutable way. We all could gaze up to the sky wondering, being just everyday people of lower intellect, these situations unequivocal fathomless irreligious incurring ingress inestimable infliction. There happens to be a omnipresent being of supernatural infusing impaling inverse infiltration knowledge that make's the world turn, without this executioner's inferring benevolence, this impish world would not turn! Gods everything, as the world turns!

Naturally, the irksome incompetent world monetary system influences indicative increasingly instability industrial impotence! Some Americans insincerely don't give an iota about identifying with correcting our American economical incredibility indirectly indisposed incorporate infirmities. Any Americanized adult should invest in foreign cars to entrust that the endorsement of the Japanese economy stays healthy? Why should Americans be inclining or ill-mannered to cause the insolvency of Japan when the incapacitating of the incorporated industrialized factories of America can be induced so inelegantly? Some people's indifference for buying foreign cars portrays the inhibitions of an inspiring trader instigator that wants to insensibly make the United States of America insolvent? The imbecilities of the U.S. auto shopper caused the imperiling impairment of U.S. factories with the incorrectness of supporting the main importer of foreign cars and ignoring the American cars! Someone told me infinitely inconclusively Japanese cars run real well, they just don't immediately stop! Good luck taking your long intrepid trip vacation with that car, remember Fred Flintstone could stop. Buy losing World War II most inartistic infatuated car shoppers would have had their dreams come true?

We won World War II only to inadvertently give every inch of our very topsoil back? All these words that we illuminated within this print, will not give anyone a hint, to where all the worldly money went? Maybe some of our incumbency of congressional multi-millionaires could use great introspection to indeed individually indulge inductive implicated investigations? Of course, we the people or subjects of this government won't impugn the impurities within the inquest of these rare insider congressional inquisitive inaccessible impropriety inextricable infamies! Maybe we could learn something illuminating from government's older incumbent introverted infidelities that have overwhelming inexcusable inelegant incubating indelible indecisions. We the people of the U.S. have our own invective inquiries like every other country of the world, except our faults are not inferior, they are superior. The only thing left to inject or inveigh within this intoxicated intimating interpretive worldly wordy exchange would be that; incidentally implications inadequate involving illiteracy!

(N-Pentament)

Those Words

I'm a novice writer notwithstanding my C average in English; hope it's unnoticeable? I passed all college English that anyone had to have for a degree. If I've learned nothing in my 60yrs of life to nurture my mind with knowledge is the only proper way to live! Who wants to ever be a nutrient nut with no way to nourish their rabid mind? Before being neutralized with neurosis, nabbed by arthritis, nailed by a train, namely my wish is to be the nattiest neighborly friend. My friends can benefit in the use of nonpareil neatness of this province linguistics! Please don't think of getting nauseous or feel like I'm nagging anyone! Anybody should be able to enjoy the novelty of this sage decorum nonsectarian narrative story with learning the (N) words the main objective. It won't be my negligence to make one radical to seize definitions or usage of a few new words.

My nucleus for writing is to naively make a number of none readers note that reading can be fun and easy. Going through high school reading was only a necessity when book reports were due. Of course everyone is neglectful and narrow-minded when young. Nobodies never wanting to foster their young minds with all the nonsense of causal reading, to maybe improve their trifle grammar! As life goes on people continually naturalize to grow older and wiser and don't get nauseated from reading. Older people want to forget about the nonessential aspects of life and focus on the much nicer nonstop nutritious learning from reading! Please enjoy this aggressive mostly nominating narrated wordy nomenclature. I don't want to be the one nominee for being the person that makes anyone's daily readings neither nominally negligible nor nefarious?

It is good to put my nightshirt on and read nightly for hours until it puts my night owl self to sleep. Nowadays reading a non-fiction book as many as 8 hours is easy, nevertheless it won't make me tired. I'm older and nonchalant being less nimble than in my younger years. I like to nestle in a nice chair and listen to a newscast on the radio watch a newsreel or maybe nimbly read a good book. At times I nod off taking a nap to rest the aged sore nape of my neck! This action helps the old nest-egg finally grow slow!

Naturally an older person normally becomes nearer to navigating their wordy worldly accomplishments nevermore. That natal notch people receive for their birthday was very noteworthy to me this year. There have been numerous times I've felt a nabbing numbness in my nippiest left hip that was broken in my car wreck! My walking life's nearness is leaving me. It's a bad time to be nose-diving, especially when necromancy tells me to sit up to write the nostrum words that we all should see, hear and understand.

That nasty car accident 22 yrs ago, when I was 38, was almost my last native navigation. Nestling on the couch for a year nursing my hip is when nameless books improved my insistent abilities to read! The nippy old pain is caused from my hip being completely shattered; it took 12 screws to put it together again. It would be normal for my nimblest self to be out nudging my friends to shoot some hoops; instead I laid at home waiting for a nurse reading a good book. Older people have nostalgic thoughts about their youth. Exercise is almost nonexistent for my bungled old body! The doctor said that 99 out of 100 died from an accident like mine! Getting nerved up about my disabled life doesn't mean that I have to act niggardly, or cooped up about it. My nominate quest to teach is nobly unbreakable! I'll give everything possible to help all! When I was nineteen years old the U.S. government paid me ninety dollars a month to fight in a war that we lost, Vietnam. Being American could cost ones nonprofit life!

So here I am the survivor avoiding neuralgia in my hip to be the one nobleman navigator trying to take the naturalizing of one's knowledge of words so many nautical miles with their final naturalization for understanding words my last national negotiation. Being a kind narrator are the words still navigable or should I nervously neglect being a caring, sharing neighbor and negotiate newly noble nonsensical notation? If ones a ne'er-do-well, who cares.

Even if people think I am a nincompoop I still have a noose on someone's attention. People needn't worry with each word ones meeting with me will narrowly get through this nirvana nightmare of human natures. For sure this nearsighted meeting might notably add some personal value to what might necessarily be needed within our lives? I'm not a nag if this story is newsy narration to be nibbled by anyone! This story is the nicest way for people to be nibbling their time away! It's very hard for one to give one a needful navigability chance to learn words for a better life. Anyone nationwide might gather a tidbit of knowledge? Maybe I could get a little nodule from this same nervousness energetic superannuated learning or teaching method we'll learn together?

There is a narrow line between being a needy naturalized genius and being nutty. Take notice that I navigate that line that often narrows to notify people for the nonce that reading is noncontiguous but it can be! Learning different words can only improve one's everyday nominated navigated intercourse with others. Either way this little node of nocturnal learning might be good nurtured news in the nick of time or maybe it could be noncommittal information to satisfy ones urges? What's expected from a northerly nutritive naïve narcissus writer with but a nook of space to expand the very nakedness to a newsier way toward ones intellectual life?

Maybe anyone could be in a group of nimbler nimrods and go to a newsstand nearby or run across the newsboy somewhere and read all the newspaper words that are seen every day. Or one could read this nest or network of words and become a noised educated notarized better person. To be sure this story will give one a nearly negotiable natty nib nicety?

What other negotiated niche can one have to nibble on Saturday night? Being 60 yrs old makes nuzzling a nymph in a negligee a nonexistent proposition for me! It would totally be against my nobility! Somebody told me that there is nitroglycerin or nutritional chemicals for old men to become noticeably younger? I'll keep my neutrality on that idea. I think this nutriment fountain of youth would be a nerving death for me. I'm negatively toward noticing any naughtiness in my old age! For sure by negligently forgetting some named drugs one's life won't be naughtier it will become so much better!

When younger I was a ninny to spend my last nickel at noisier nightclubs in town finishing with a nightcap most nights. I used nicotine avidly and drank with the noisiest bar hoppers in the nation. Doing it all for naught with really a careless carefree attitude toward what my needs or aspirations for life were! Nowise do I smoke anymore and won't ever figure out why I did for the nothingness of it all? Smoke got into my eyes while reading which necessitated that I quit smoking, amen! Those days with bar napkins heavy drinking are long gone, amen! Yet, nary will many days pass before a little ale is consumed by me to compensate for the nippier pain in my left hip! A little wine to merry the soul?

In this present day and age times have changed. Forever I'll try to neurotically nationalize to do what is good for society. I'm out of neutral and enjoying my nattier life that is in gear. Forever I'll be trying to build up my nerve to give the neediest people something that might necessitate them to nudge their lives into gear also without taking a nethermost nosedive? Please don't think I'm nettling into anyone's lives, writing is a way to relieve my neuroses to correct my life! If my notions were to nettle into the lives of others it wouldn't coalescence with my calm elderly life. My neuritis will be nullified to relieve its own pain if nationalizing the nuzzled teaching of a little nicer something to the neediness of anyone is accomplished in broad daylight or nocturnally!

Anyone could be on narcotics like the namby-pamby ninnies being seen from noon until the rooster crows? The naked truth is that nobody knows the name of any doctor that prescribed the nomads their drugs and I wasn't about to get nosey. I'll just keep numbly noiseless avoiding needling with the incivilities of those nomadic idiots. There are enough pains in the necessities to nourishing my life already. Who wants to be on the negative side of noisily nonplus negotiating with drug dealers? Even with nearsightedness the omnipresent nipping drug dealer is easy to see! I've noticed dealers neutralizing neighbors wherever these nonresident dealers might go nullifying the secure sanity within yet another hood!

Most drug dealers are of different nationalities. The drug dealers I've seen remind me of the Neanderthal, oh what an intelligent breed of people! Their notoriety allows them to nonchalantly go to any corner to sell or receive a dose of drugs. Some people have their own nurseries at home to grow their own! People don't have to needlessly wear the nipples off their new tires to find drugs. The drugs are probably right next-door? The naughtiest people could do without drugs, but these nuts can't get a natural high that reading a good book will give anyone else. They probably can't read? Nay the education they received was numerically how to buy and sell newfangled fancy drugs one nugget at a time which is very nauseating. I feel a little nausea coming on like when I think of the Nazarene or Jews the people born in Nazareth! These people were killed by the Nazi or Nazism. Hitler was the sickest man that ever lived! Drug dealers are just as sick slowly killing all kid's of every nationality with their nonchalance barbarism!

The druggie may take something into the needier parts of their bodies. It's in the mouth or up the nasal cavity or a little needlework to shoot up, not into the brain for any goodness and it probably is noticeable? They think their needled lives are dull but with nicknames like Nitro their lives are null and void! Being noncombatant I don't get to nosy watching their nastiest actions. I want to neatly live my life too! There isn't any way my affairs will be nudged into the affairs of drug dealers! I don't have the nerves for noisy nagged nonplussing negotiations with the nastiness of drug dealer's crooked narrowness appalling contacts with others!

There is plenty of nervous young people whose nature of education is nil or totally forgotten, what's happening nationally everyday! The marijuana the nurseryman grows deforms the nominal growth of the nursery school child's parent's brains? No-one gets a proper education anymore and this negation causes nonstop corruption to run rampant in the neighborhoods! Drug dealing is a great notable nonpartisan neighboring nonconformity nemesis that has to be eradicated.

My North American city is the murder capital of the U.S.A., what's drug's got to do with this numerated naturalness? Newark, New Jersey is a golden nimbus compared to the noisiness of gunfire around my northern city? What numbers or names can be notified to nail the coffin shut on these nerve-racking novelties of death so that it doesn't linger any longer than need be? What about nationalism to have drug dealings nipped down to a minimum with the nimbleness of proper government. This might help nurturing the crime rate to be nursed back to a healthy neighborliness level?

The National Guard might be nosing in if this city could just hit the proper magical enumerating numeral for deaths!? My city had to lay off 25% of the police force last week the strangest numerical nuttiest nub of this very fine story. It makes me numb that the government can be so dumb! I'm noting police brutality or the lack of it? The nonexistence or nullification to the police force notoriously gives crime a fighting chance? Life can't get nuttier unless the police leave for nonpayment of their services?

Forensic science, the study of dead bodies and crime is the only notifying nonunion open job left within this city. These trained people have to study the bullets pulled from the numerating corpse that lie around town! Most people would think the study of the nationalist lives and liberties of the nice people of the U.S.A. would be the most popular nicely netted jobs, wrong! It is a novel idea to have a steady growing job to be able to study the horrible deaths and destructions that are naughtily near here all around this corrupt town! Can anyone clear this nebulas mess up to let everyone see the nodding lighter brighter finer side of life?

Drug dealing is the only nationalistic namesake way to have nepotism within the lives of native-born poor families, necessitating it hard to get rid of! The nonentities of nominees are brothers teaching brothers while uncles teach nieces and nephews so everyone gets an equal netting of the profits, especially after nightfall. This is how the nighthawk dealers get nomination to work the nightly family plan within the neighborhood, very nebulous?

Newborn laws let many needless nonconformists get medical marijuana and needles are free. This might help a numerate few disabled people for sure. Some naturalist could also give official notification that net corruption is the norm. Of course the newness of society will be full of nearby nadir naughty negligent numskulls. This forms nettled hardships to this ever shrinking drug free society that have to be corrected and nailed to the wall.

Since I'm nowhere a noted novelist or a notary this would nullify my abilities to notarize a notebook or make any noise for the next nationalized legislation of drug laws. Being a newcomer neophyte novitiate is kind of nattily since I'm through with my nerve-wracking neurotic behavior. I'm nerveless to continue without that last nip of that nondescript nectar that's in my noggin? This will really cause my neutralization in a nonproductive way unless it is non-alcoholic? I used to drink and be a numberless nonentity notorious noxious nuisance. This is why I say in a nutshell, Noetic Notion . . . nourishment necessary now!

(G Pentanment)

Childs Courtesy

Thanks for taking time from the fun of gaming or whatever one's gamesome gumption may be to grapple with this glorious generous guaranteed gradual glossary! One can always find a dictionary to be a guide for great generative knowledge. I'm a gambler that this little story will be bridging the gap to garner new genuine words, that aren't grandiloquent? Just maybe one will become a galvanic guy or gal that knows? Please take a gander at this glimpsing story gesturing sage reverence to the gender of everyone! Generally graceful guidance to a genteel life is to be generated gallantly with a good graduating education! My gamblers idea has been gravitated or glued to the glutinous garnishment appointment of our get-together within the glories of this glut story! I'm the gladdest one if this glutting story is used as the glossiest gauge to reading alright?

When I was knee high to a grass-hopper growing up, an adult could whip their children or grand-children with twigs or tree branches. I know for a grisly fact it could be done from my graduation of this discipline. My whippings whipped gloss into the gallantries of my manners as I grew. With my guarded gesture from my visits with this grislier gauntlet with the switch my germinating generousness of manners had a stout guidepost! My manners were switched to gainfully excel generosity into my gentile body and brain. I could never forget the corrective actions of the basic generalization of my gloomier thoughts for this grisliest form of correction! The switch grooming theory germinated my manners into perfect shape, it stuck on me forever!

My immediate genealogy or genetics was gotten or instilled by the switch. If I didn't say yes sir, no sir, yes mam, no mam, grand-pa and grand-ma would wear the gnarls off the weeping willow tree branches. Granny's intense gesticulation broke two branches on me more than once while I growled in minor pain! I had a gut feeling to be completely a glutton for unlimited fine gloried courtesies! Sparing the switch will spoil the grubby child. I still don't know if that old weeping willow tree got its name generalized from the graveness of my whippings or weeping?

I grieve present day children that have the ghastly manners of morons, which is gross! The guideline for teaching children moral values is null and void almost gone, there should be a guidebook. Having a guest over for a visit might be a graved kind of grimmest situation. If their giddy child glides through the house and finally breaks something gracelessly with their gangling gait, all a person can do is gulp in guiltless shame. With gut wrenching grief a person has to gravely grumble to grunt grinding their teeth to forget about grabbing the child to correct them for their giddiest wild behavior! Adults might want grips on the kid's gullets or to whack that frail backside one time? Even if the adult were to gracefully correct the child's gawkiness, the adult would be found guilty. The world is full of giggling galloping children that will give adults gastric pains from their actions! New laws make the discipline of children a gambled situation!

Adults don't even want to graze the kid on the behind with a backhand or they would be grabbed up in front of a grand-jury? Gosh the only piece of wood seen in this story would be the judge's gavel? This would be a perfect time to gladly grin and bear it! It's grotesquely obscene the way children are greatly gravitating toward a complete glaring glummest ghoulish failure!

Gee a gawky grade-school child won't have a gram of generic etiquette like I received. To generalize that one has to have a glimpse of glister in their lives to relieve the gloominess isn't an understatement! I believe the kids of today have a ghostly genie guardian watching over all their guilt? If children had a gifted governess teaching them pleasant gracing they could be goaded into greathearted good-humored children. Most adults today don't have the getup to teach or greenback in order to pay someone to grill and teach Godspeed courtesy to their grumbler kids!

Gentlefolk have to develop true grit to take giant steps to try generically doing away with all the grayish ghoulishness in young lives. One has to feel guiltless gripping the grittiest talents one can receive guaranteeing to have a fruitful comfortable life. Why live a grimly gremlin life when one could take out the guesswork to have gripped a glorified life with godsend galvanizing glean. One's life can be ground into its glassiest gleaner perfection with just a basic germ of friendship!

What kind of germicide will remove the gaping graven glazing of the child's gentlest bad moral fibers? A gardener might girdle the lives of some garnering the commendable garnish of the gawkiest children into shape like a garden that grows a wonderful harvest? The glazed germs of greenhorn kids today are to corrupt for any kind of grappled gadget to repair the grimacing of the huge gash of gracelessness gall with any amount of courteous generating pleasant grating?

A guillotine or gibbet gallows would be a terrible getaway to say goodbye to the gabby grated gusher mouths of the immature giddier teenagers. These would all be godless inhuman corrections to the problem, guillotining isn't a proper form of guardianship! Commonsense is a guarantor that gladden generalship guiding to lead children from a greenish childhood to the gracefulness of adulthood has to come from the genially of gladsome compassionate adult mentors with the assistants of proper generation. A randomly short glimpsed greeting of this charitable gladness giveaway has to be able to help make one a friendly gladiator for life?

Golly I'd be glad if the young adults could gratuitously lose all the gibing grime and nasty garbage in their gauntly lives? The glared grossness of the gabbiest gabbling teenagers gibe talk makes gagging seem very pleasant! Have I mentioned the gratings at the guard-house of the state prison are geometrical and made of granite and a grille grid of gratings! I know one caught the gist of the grimness of that gasping sentence? This is where the non-disciplined grimy grudging child will graduate from. That is if they aren't groomed by a guardian generator of knowledge to make the grade or grandeur when they are grown! To avoid groaning or grimacing about that glummer grimmer situation adults have to greedily gather the time to make sure the gruff gaunt children are graciously grooved to glide into goodhearted honest, caring, sharing adults. The guaranties that the generality of a descent life are granulated into one will have to come from a gaily glancing glorification glossy glow from a dedicated graybeard grandee gunning to improve someone's life for the best! A few years of gushed grammar schooling won't hurt grammatically!

Thank God I know my grandson and grand-daughter still mind their girding manners. They have been guided to almost the same goodwill grooving manners that I was graced with! Being courteous is genealogical if given when you switch your manners to the grindstone for geniality. My genealogies receive discipline to grant their goodly gala gorgeous golden goals!

If everyone in this world was gingerly and said, thank you, you're welcome and so on, this simple grandiloquence would help people sticking or gluing together. Gratuitous common conversation with the gang at work gave genial gusto companionship to us every day we were together. At times our general conversation was complete garble gibberish with just a grain of meaning. Sometimes we would be in the groove and have heart to heart conversations with a glimmer of meaning, instead of just gossip. The glory of these gliding glittery conversations was gorgeously something to goggle at, a fantastic glared gas! The local gazette has but a granule of knowledge compared to the giantess glassy gossipy gathered talks we shared in the shop! The glib intelligent talks glowed giving me the most gracious graphic gainful gravitational growth!

The gentlemen at work were a gem of knowledge for the good-natured gentle gregarious person I am. I had been brought up with strict morals to respect the generosities of my elders at all times. Anytime was the right time to gravitate my etiquette enjoying having them as my generalizing courteous mentors without many gripes or complaints? The people at work had a gimmick to use the gift of gab in generously teaching the golden-rule. Sometimes these people used their genera intelligence of practiced glibness to expand a certain point with a glance of wise smoothness making it so hard to comprehend! Most of the people working with me were older; I guessed grand-fathers and grand-mothers. Ironically someone's grandparent was to be gratefully guilty of teaching me the guise of becoming a glaringly gleeful gamboled grownup.

I enjoyed talking to my fellow workers never really having a grievance to gainsay their wondrous conversations. Year after year they gently were my gild girded generators of the basic girdled gust of knowledge to gaining proper etiquette in my life! The galleries of the guild with these workers added the finniest granulating gallantry to my polite adult life. Talking to these wise people took the guesswork out of what way my life was to be guided with a gush of gratis gilding. Gauging that life is short and sweet, the glossier gold way is the best glamour way to glorify the genuineness of life with a garnet of perfection instilled into a gold-filled pure life!

I would use conversation with the guileful elderly people in order to grind perfection into my basic gambit etiquette of continuing my adult life. Some gestures that were gesticulated in the shop were of groundless information in garnishing the germination of my young mind! I had to make sure to grasp onto the proper etiquette and grammar. Who wants the glumness to gnaw into their life's from the geyser gale of cussing and swearing from grossly used vulgar language?

My thoughts or morals weren't gauged by groggier garrulous giggly conversations. The gabbier giggled chatter was like radiation to me! If the gabble or gibber got to intense this would goad my Geiger counter gene to look somewhere else for my goal of learning respectful clean courteous friendship! Anytime the talk got gaudy I had to go. I always avoided lingering to become the gainer of the old grumpy grouchy gyrating grotesque guttural they gunned at me!

Government control does regulate how people of the world react to each other with a gravity of special gratitude. In the Middle Eastern countries there would be a gigantic gasp of horror if a woman's face and body are not gartered with a gauzy gown or veil type material. The girls of America wear tiny bikinis, garters or any garb. The geisha girls of Japan are almost the same as American dancers except for their garlands and other garments made of gossamer or silk that only a true goddess would wear! This is only one glancing difference to governing people.

Any geographer of this world could tell of the gushing variety of graver different major customs. When I was a child if I got caught gnawing at my food not saying grace I couldn't have any goulash! I'd always end up groveling in a glummer shame to gurgling about being hungry and finally dad let me eat leftovers! These minor actions of authority guarded me from being a gluttonously gourmand for too much food in my present daily life! All actions in one's life direct the important guards of character that one will have to garrison to have an improved moral life! To be a goalkeeper covered by the greatest gauges of the geniuses for a moral life one has to keep away from the gauntness ghastliness of a filthy corruptible life! Granted each worldly country, state, county, city, family, person are different entities that have their own geography laws to grow onward or govern them with! Stick to the grandness magic plan to do what is right!

In the old gayness of America there isn't much gradation of laws from state to state. The simple gapping laws change slightly, as long as one is not a speeder or into drugs, one should be most gratified? I found out that there are grave greedy people in each and every state. Being an old gullible man it is sometimes hard to guard against being gypped. Some people want to gratify their garish gentry by charging double for food items! When the grocer says 5 dollars for the gallon of milk that I could have for 2 dollars at the grocery store in my state that is total greed and an outrage to me! I had to grovel and groan in my gloom and say, thank you? This was the pure common gearing courtesy that has been girdling around me since I was a gamboling child. I was courteous and the getter of a offset with a goofy good-sized grumbling glumly grudge.

Anyone would have to grimace in a gusty shock at the store for the gouged price of the milk, cookies and garlic potato chips. I still thanked him in the glibbest way for gouging or gypping me for the grub! I'm a frugal happy shopper not wanting to be gluttonous and grab any gourmet goodies to maybe gobble. I finally grudgingly left that store with my goods in a glum only to gnash my teeth, grunting feeling my groggiest from the complete greediness of the store!

I'm only human and when I give my greetings and goodbyes they will always be polite even when getting gored at this greedier store, there would have been gratuity if it was at all applicable. Small gratuities have been left by my grouchiest self before because of lousy service! Being human without many complaints, my unwanted grouchiness is sometimes followed by some very bad minor glanced gesticulating that was accidentally grilled into me at the shop! I went through my grouchier gamut of vulgar feelings from the gull of the lousy cheating store clerk. Feeling gritty I could have become a gambling gamester and galloped into the ghetto to greet a gangster and gained a grandly deal from the grumpiest greediest guiltiest goriest gunman?

This grand globe we live on is a giant glorifying geographical society godly gad gallery gathering gratification of this galaxy. We are not all famous gleamed brilliant people. Everyone could maybe gradually use a little glint of groundwork to gear them to a goodlier glisten in a world of graveled dull and boring people! Most of us groom our lives to gallivant daily being gadabouts playing a game. It is okay to gambol about pulling gags having fun as long as one is polite doing it. Keeping people happy and gay will be the alighting way to germinate ones day!

Don't gloat in glory for being a grueling grouch or glower. I guess being grumpy is okay if it doesn't last all day and if ones not gossiping badly about the good-looking acts or actions of others. Graciousness always receives a gifted greeter's welcome more then the giver of a gripe! The terrible garishly gadding gadflies are too gruff for any warm hearted Good Samaritan maybe teaching them the reverence courteous life of the morally righteous that is more than any growl!

Life would be better to live in a greenness grasser glen full of beautiful flowers then setting in a guttered barren gulf with nothing but gypsy-moths, glowworms, gnats, Gila monsters and roaches eating almost everything in sight! It is wonderful knowing one's life could be so beautiful in a field filled with geraniums, gardenias and gentians which in order are red, white and blue flowers that looks like OLD GLORY making one feel amazed of one's gentle human behavior as a courteous girl or gent! Ones gearshift manners and American flag flower field could make goose pimples rise from its mental gyration grandiose splendor! While getting gazed gentleness from this sight one could stand in front of the General Assembly of the U.S.A. and be proud that one is a caring citizen doing a good turn to governor their lives without guiltiness!

One should never want to be a gorged gibbon or gorilla caught up in the gullies or grounds of life grazing the gnarled infected galls or graft instead of the gamey greensward field to share with all humanity! Think about the wonders of a gentler glad life full of glee instead of grimacing about all the sowed seed of graceless hatred. I don't have to be Galileo to generalize the gullibility of kid's or the little goblins nowadays are revolving around with grimaced jerk jive talking friends to swerve them in the wrong direction. The world needs honest, courteous gritted kids grounding for a decent society in the future and grandsires, goodwives or mothers for life?

Being in the grassland full of goldenrod, gladiolus or any fraternal gritting field of life is the best way to nourish one's life! While in this potent geology greenery field one could look up to see the pretty birds, robins, eagles, doves, grosbeaks, grouse, gull and of course guinea fowl, grebe, gander, geese, gobblers and the little gosling that run through the field! Little children walking into the barren fields of briers will be in the gravest condition to be granulated by the tainted nourishment glare of dominate vices instead of the purity from correct resolving ginger virtues into their lives. When they look up to see birds, they will see vultures, goshawks, hawks, grackle, ravens and gamecocks or any bird living with this genetic ghastlier infliction! Vultures are where these kids will resign on the graph for working in this society! I don't think this grouping of children can compel to have many inspirational C.E.O.s? A geologist studying this land will only see rats, spiders and garter snakes not any furry little bunnies, groundhogs or gophers! A grudging manner less life is like living in the Gobi desert without greens or a glass or a gourd of water to guzzle! The forlorn graces of this graveling life would be full of grieved despair. The soul purpose for this grubbiest life is to find a graveyard or gravestone, no guided missile for a long life here! With mannerisms life wouldn't be tough goings. It would be smooth and easy like lightly greased gravy, filled with companionships or relationships instead of gory.

The guile of most barren kids walking into the guzzling gorging geologic fields of filth won't help them relish life with glider manners. They will have to bustle grievously through the imp thorniest fields or gutters and gulches of life that infect or fill them with contempt! They will tend to be granulated so full of the glandular thoughts and ideas of corruption that no disinfectant germicidal cleansing curing can ever resolve the grubbier graving gore gapping gummed up gilt!

Too bad these gamin kids don't have a gnome near some home to glare over their gushy gobbled gelatin lives that supply less nourishing griefless firmness stability than a frail ice cube in a sweltering summer heat! Life is better to gallop into a grove of greenwood trees then to walk by the goggling distraction of the deserted desolate detachment from the sights of a gaped row of vacant ghostlier homes ready to be grazed! Get one's life in gearwheel order and blossom like an old oak tree with acorns. Don't be the geological vandal tree being used abused and will have to eventually be torn down or destroyed with plenty of grower life left. Don't live life in vain without using ones brain. Be a gladiatorial respectable person with a consecrated charisma that has dignity and pride to gage ones sights gauged above the horizon to foretell a galvanizing life is a girder prescription fashion for life! Don't let vices overwhelm ones governable virtuous life.

One could be a gypsy to find a glorying gratifying gangway toward the girth of a gateway to gather a genesis to the glossiness of suppliant knowledge! The handles to proper life and fine etiquette are always available just grope them? If one could groom their gaze to the right gate and not gawk at the astonishing genius one could be, then this would be the gentility glitter for all humanity! With any group of people there's a guaranty that a percentage is going to be geared for grievous graceless gruesome glaring griping? One has to avoid a gibe grudged griming life to grip a saintly life without gaudier gimcrack or gewgaw to show off what nobody needs to know!

If people around the globe were all alike, this world would be a grim groggy gloomy global gorge! With the greatness of a well greasing difference in people genuinely the goodliness will seem to gleam with an array of godlike groveled go-betweens. To tell the way people of the earth are graphically now days is like grappling with a grab-bag, we are not sure what goodness is in them and hopefully they are good-tempered. We all could gain gaiety girt galore if we could galvanize our gospel common grateful courteous generalities. The genus of the human being allows for one's grasping gleaming glowing glamorous given unlimited glossy glossaries!

(O-pentament)

B.P. and Me

For almost two months now nobody's optimistic overall opinion occurs occasionally. How can anyone have a good outlook for what the future may bring from the oddness that has two million gallons absolute crude petroleum obscenely gushing into the ocean every day? This objectionable man-made oil well might never stop leaking. What impact will this owe upon the sterling delicate odorous balance of nature? Every day the obstinacies about this outrageous leak continue sea plants and animals are dying from this occasion's overdosed offender. Countless millions upon millions of sea creatures are dying including whales, porpoise, clams, oysters and octopuses and all fish. Land animals and their offspring are dying. Broods of birds like the osprey, seagulls, pelicans and every creature and organism within miles are dying!

Oh what magical kind operational orchestration can be done to outwitting this crucial crude crude ecological environmental oppression? There should be systematic options owing to fixing the petroleum leaks originated before any actual drillings ever began? Maybe some magic occult powers could be obsequious in deleting the sight from this ugly gusher spill that is not an optical illusion that has to be put in the offing A.S.A.P. As long as the known gas companies are making money who cares? Somehow we have to organize an obtruded way to outwear the oddities from this corrupt leak ruining lives for plenty that isn't an overstatement!

The auto manufactures obviously made brakes to stop cars. The origination for the light switch was to control the lights. What obscuring observations could be had if the faucet wasn't invented completely omitting water control flow? It does seem as though there should be a systematic outstanding orderly outline to overcome this out-of-the-way crude ecological obstacle. The petroleum gushers should have an orientate value organizing petroleum control flow. With the omission for objective systematic gusher control the future for the waters around the world looks bleak. The petroleum olfactory will linger even if someone can out-guess "Mother Nature" to obliterate this offensive leaky gusher. It will take an obscured undesirable time to recover the shimmering effervescent odoriferous opalescent deep blue waters of the sea!

The petroleum spill has overflowed inland and with the hurricane season here opportunities to carry the petroleum overland will increase which could contaminate fresh water everywhere. Our government should have ordered optimum open-handed help from the onset to make sure this environmental disaster is obliterated. Instead they became onlookers not wanting to overdo maybe overreach their omnipotent governmental powers. Most petroleum drillings outlets goodness otherwise greatly outweighs this outright outspread overgrown outflow outrage. Where is that originator officiating adviser that can begin outstripping this terrible leaking mess? Everyone would be overjoyed to overhear that the gusher has been obviated and capped. The overall observing outlook offers very little strict orderlies for suggestions to fix this petroleum gusher's obscene overwhelming output that has to be outwitted by man and osculated goodbye!

With simple observation any oaf knows that the officiated obligatory organization was obscure throughout these whole obnoxious crude offensively overworked oppressions stay. The government should have been overcrowding B.P.'s opprobrious personal to procure surety obviating the ooze. When the waters became over-coated super oily from the onrush leaking by offshore drillings the harmful effects could not have been overestimated!

The government should feel obligated and be in overdrive to obtrude into B.P.'s petroleum outraging affairs to obviate this obvious unhealthy occurrence against all oceanic organisms. The plants and animals are dying because they can't get any oxygen. This whole mess seems like one bad omen with B.P.'s overtaxed personal working useless overtime trying to control this odysseys encumbrance. The U.S. government is overestimating it to be an easy fix!

Somehow there has to be an opiate way that maybe an outspoken ombudsman can find a way to outshine everyone and find the oblique organ to turn off this oiliness disaster! It shouldn't offend the officials and owners at B.P. if the U.S. government was offering friendly overbearing or any off-shoot old-fashioned brotherly assistants in obliterating this odious oddity against all humanity. B.P. and the U.S. government should combine using open-minded oneness and their obtrusive overwrought opulence in an original way to out-do each other to overtake this obese outstretching national ecological disaster before it is an overseas ecological disaster.

Originally this one-sided petroleum leak should have opened oncoming opportune optional orientation between government and overloaded private business. In the first place B.P. should have a systematic outlying orientating plan for the oppressive out-come operation to oppose the out-and-out outburst from a broken overrun well. Somehow B.P. and the U.S. government ominously overlooked the possibility that the orient for a strict systematic fix for a crude gusher eruption would ever be needed? The U.S. government should have been the main overseer observer to overshoot B.P.'s authority to convene initial outgoing operative beginning engineering. Why has the gas companies often operated without any overshadowing government opposition? The onward openings for new wells was oblivious not overly observable to the very obloquies obtuseness of the U.S. governments control, they didn't want to go overboard with.

Now the government has to openly take an optic look to observe more than occasional overnight petroleum drilling. Government should have been occupying themselves with their obligations and been government observant with the gas company's many gusher overproductions. Instead the obscurity of this government was performing obliging favors for gas companies not taking offense in thinking this obstructed tragedy we have now would ever happen! Now the U.S. government might have to build an observatory or observatories to watch what will happen in the aftermath for this overdose leak that should have been fixed by now?

Someone in the government (E.P.A.) office, maybe some caring old omnibus officeholder with governmental olive branch pentagon experience might oblige to find an instant onslaught to oppress this overstayed oiliest mess. We have to find the right opponent to outclass this problem and be opposite against the plentiful opportunist that are governmental officers orchestrating to fix this mess and stand up for an ovation. Somehow all the people in charge have to move onwards to outstrip onerous people to ordain a fix for this overspread environmental crude overdosing. This obstruct environmental overloading can't be overestimated! Can any open-eyed intelligent under oath person that won't ogle at it, find the means to the omega fix to wear down the overbalanced obesity outdoor ecological disaster that can't get much oilier?

I'm obstinate in my overtly objections that the government should have obtained an opinionated organic systematic ordinary way to overhaul a leaking gusher before any initial drillings? It is an odd offset objectivity to make fixing the leaking gusher an encumbered maybe obtainable occupational occasion? How could have the gas companies omitted the opportunity to learn how to cap gushers when the outset for gusher drillings were first under development, what idiots? There should be one-way at least to overbalance a crude gusher before it is drilled by the gusher opener? The government from the outside could have become obsequiously officiators to make crude gusher ownership overtures in fixing the gushers part overhead in the final outward outlay laws and regulations for the openness of B.P.'s continuous overawed well drillings!

What opulent outlandish means ought to outgo the outfitting to oust this terrible occurring outcry that we've gotten ourselves involved with? There should have been an observed understandable preventive maintenance to control this corruptible ominous offal petroleum waste that has an oozed obstructive outgrow occupancy to the coasts in all the southern United States.

The obloquy from the fishermen that fish everyday for a living is understandable since they are outrageously unable to outrun the oversupplying of crude from the gusher and are left in oblivion. The waters in these southern states make the occurred incurring thoughts to continue fishing an obsolete obsession. They must all obligate to stay home and hope and pray that the great obtruding oozing obstinacy obstruction will not ruin their already oppressed livelihoods. At least fisherman in overalls that are omnivorous can't eat any seafood and can knock it from their open-faced diet! The spill has already become an opaque obsessed oscillating overcharged obscenity. If the leaks finally fixed there will be an orgy from the exciting outbreak grandeur from its overhauling.

The old-timer fishermen have to be obedient and stay home to obey what the octagon shaped stop sign from the U.S. government says and aren't able to object! They are all hoping their outcries for their jobs won't become obsolescent. Their lives have all changed offhand and are at odds to ever change in the near obscuring future. They hope to outlast, maybe outlive this horrifying adventures overstay and can't wait for its obliteration to be stuck in the next obituary? Maybe B.P. can get outfitted to outfox "Mother Nature". If they overthrew this oversized out-of-door mess they won't have to be ostracized by the entire obstreperous outlying fishermen's group. The fishermen are praying B.P. and maybe the U.S. government will fix this petroleum's sickening ocular sight that seems to be way beyond repair! It's in a titanic stupor orbit by itself?

An oversized problem like this could override omnipresent government's overruling to overthrow this situation. It might take an intelligent omniscient oracular outsider to overstep to oversee why the B.P.'s overrated scientist can't fix this odium overburdened crude ecological disaster. This crude overhanging overcast ecological problem can't be overstated and is long overdue to be overpowered by man. It shouldn't take an ogling octave from eight men to figure how to fix this oldest ungodly odyssey that has been racking miles upon B.P.'s work odometer!

What obstinately outdated laws and regulations are in effect toward the occupied blest obedience operating for gas companies drilling? Who knows, with their obduracy they must work under their own laws and out-of-date regulations? Money talks and everyone that might be without walks! The gas company is above everything, at least over the "Laws of Nature". What about the overlooked gloomy overcastting for the future lives for all the overclouded plants and animals upon this overwhelmed earth, time will tell? With people even the osteopathic, maybe the working ossifying obstetrician might have to obligate their professions to find a new opine difference with their obstetrics when delivering new born babies! The ladies ovaries, ovum could be infected from overeating the petroleum spills seafood that the women might have consumed?

Felling my oats I should obliquely go ahead to be the ogre organizer to dig an outlawed gusher in my backyard without obeying regulation? Then again maybe I shouldn't dig outdoors since I received a ticket once for working in my outbuilding with my son. I had broken an established outmoded ordinance against working on cars at home. I only wish I had any gas company's authority to do whatever whenever wherever I want without obligating laws to cover my ongoing affairs? My yard will look good with an ostensibly ostentatious osmosis oasis okay?

Being a stout objector my overt officious would be for B.P. to drill two more wells in an outer proximity to overlap the gusher that is leaking. These wells would release the outermost pressure from the oversupplying opposing well. Their organized overlapping pressure release will be offsetting to outdistance the obscenities already being received from the crude wells overproduction from this man-made gusher? I'm not going to try outselling the ideas of the plentiful crude scientists that are not able outdistancing this outdoor unmanageable mess. This is my idea as a semi-intelligent outfielder trying to outplay this out-of-doors problem to bring back overbalancing overawing normalcy to this oddly corruptible relentless incubus petroleum spill? There has to be a way to ordain an orderliness superior fix to this outgrown ecological disaster?

Soon someone will have to write the opus obverse ode to this oils ungodly humongous mess! Everyone could go to the gulf to watch this operatic accursed death and destruction that is running now and will probably end up the longest running opera ever? The crude leak is not an operetta for sure! To make sure people receive the maximum horrific espousers bring your opera glasses! Most people in the southern U.S.A. don't have an optimistically good attitude about life!

The ships that are in the Gulf of Mexico making their daily outings are not pleasure ships. The ships are working outriggers with huge sponges being pulled along to outflank this mess and suck up the sludge from the deluging gusher! It would be wonderful if the U.S. government could have helped to outfit this gushers leaking to put a stop to it! This would give them a reason to ostentatiously show the openwork from a giant Old Glory to fly in the open-air! With all considerations this kind gesture would show the U.S. government cares for the American people and the ossification for cleaning the waters around the world? Who knows if this old-maidish government really cares about most poor working people at all? There doesn't seem as though anyone is ready to overcrowd B.P. for the proper fix of this definite demonic organic deluge?

It's not an overestimate that it will take a while before anyone gets the opportunity to take a lovely long pleasurable outboard motor outing in the Gulf of Mexico, ouch! My opined consensus is that the financial and ecological loses from this crude outbreak are much greater than anyone could ever imagine? So far all operations that have been tried to fix this mess have completely failed? When the spill reaches the Occident maybe the more intelligent Occidental government will formulate a fix to overhaul this organically uncontrollable mess that definitely has a terrible odor . . .

Somehow man will have to have perseverance to outwit this opposed man-made nature's overawe orifice and overmaster to become the operator onto what should be ours. It will take intelligent ordinarily orotund people with optimist attitudes to become ornamental orators to orchestrate originating oversight overturning this outraged oil ordeal!

To whom it may concern:

Hello my name is Jack Flick a 60yr old retired G. M. electrician. I spent 164 credit hrs, at Mott Community College over the last 40yrs failing to receive a degree. During 2010 I've tried to make up for my lack of education by taking 2500hrs abridging the," Webster's New World Dictionary" with Student Handbook (1981). A-BINGO is the six letters that have been condensed or consumed into six unusual, uncommon, and unheard of educational short stories using most the words from the dictionary that can be used to make sense within the mule stories! These short stories are only MULES that carry the words that one should know. Eight hours to read 21,000 words of entertaining intellectual information. Do I have your overall attention yet?

My (A-pentament), "Educational Encouragements" has approximately 3,500 words with 1,200 different A words without repetition. My idea is for everyone to kick back and read the dictionary instead of being amazed by what is in it. Educational Encouragements is a good 40 minutes of reading that will introduce anyone to almost every A word they will ever need to know for LIFE! The idiomatic stories, or MULES, are a fair way to instill knowledge into one that wants to learn! Has your curiosity been activated or do you think I'm extremely cuckoo?

To introduce this six chapter book to 10th grade students would show the words needed to significantly increase neologism or the passion for learning? My manuscript's magnificent mule magnetism mesmerizes (M-pentament) the college student's fanatical fantasies as they read in wonder and amazement with high-school students they think it's a very unusual scrupulously interesting incredible impossible unbelievable godly way to write!

I would faithfully appreciate your authorized official approval for my persistent ability to condense the dictionary before I perish? Being an old crippled Vietnam Vet gives me plenty of righteous time to write. I would cordially invite your superior wisdom or writing abilities to condone or condemn the future printing of this book? If I could inconvenience you to please take time to read my idea for education I would gladly send the title page, preface, introduction and a excerpt from a (mule story), for your scholarly opinionated inspection. I have started the H's with enthusiastic vigor to educate the children of America in the only way I know. In my (I-pentament), "World Peace" the word I is used just once, the very first word of 2,800, with 750 different I words, never within any pentament, (mule story), is a word that starts with that specific letter repeated! I managed to use I 12 times in this paragraph! Reading used to be dull and boring, not anymore. The alliteration of these words should incite neologism.

Yours truly lost for words,

Sage reverence wise guy Jack

P.S. I had an extreme inspirational headache when writing the introduction (April1st, 2010). It was the first words in print that now control my never ending religious attempt to do something for society before I say goodbye.

PENTAMENT—primordial prose that includes the original concept conclusive concentrated consecutive conjunction of five words alphabetically aphaeresis, alliteration void repetition.

Printed in the United States
by Baker & Taylor Publisher Services